CREATING A COMPREHENSIVE INFORMATION LITERACY PLAN

A How-To-Do-It Manual and CD-ROM for Librarians

Joanna M. Burkhardt
Mary C. MacDonald
Andrée J. Rathemacher

**HOW-TO-DO-IT MANUALS
FOR LIBRARIANS**

NUMBER 150

NEAL-SCHUMAN PUBLISHERS, INC.
New York, London

Published by Neal-Schuman Publishers, Inc.
100 William St., Suite 2004
New York, NY 10038

Printed and bound in the United States of America.

The paper used in this publication meets the minimum requirements of American National Standard for Information Sciences—Permanence of Paper for Printed Library Materials, ANSI Z39.48—1992. ∞

Library of Congress Cataloging-in-Publication Data

Burkhardt, Joanna M.
  Creating a comprehensive information literacy plan : a how-to-do-it manual and CD-ROM for librarians / Joanna M. Burkhardt, Mary C. MacDonald, Andree J. Rathemacher.
    p. cm. — (How-to-do-it manuals for librarians ; no. 150)
  Includes bibliographical references and index.
  ISBN 1–55570–533–2 (alk. paper)
    1. Information literacy—Study and teaching (Higher)   2. Library orientation—Planning.   3. Communication in information science.   I. MacDonald, Mary C. II. Rathemacher, Andrée J.   III. Title.   IV. How-to-do-it manuals for libraries; no. 150.

ZA3075.B868 2005
028.7—dc22   2005013719

CONTENTS

LIST OF WORKSHEETS

PREFACE

A comprehensive information literacy plan offers proof positive that an institution is committed to equipping its students with all the skills necessary for survival in the information age. An effective plan provides a means and method for achieving delivery. It addresses and incorporates the needs of students, faculty, and staff—and delivers a clear message to important members of the academic community, including directors, university presidents, deans, boards of governors, alumni, prospective students and their parents, and many more. A successful approach looks outward, demonstrating the importance and centrality of the library to education. It must also work internally to organize instruction and facilitate the creation of courses, keep individuals and working teams on track, aid in resource allocation, and gauge progress and identify areas for improvement.

Creating a Comprehensive Information Literacy Plan: A How-to-Do-It Manual for Librarians helps turn this important task into a "doable" process by identifying small, manageable steps. Its four-step framework will guide planners, writers, and instructors in creating a plan with a wide-ranging program that meets the needs and audiences of their particular institution and features real-world implementations.

ORGANIZATION

Part I, "Creating a Comprehensive Information Literacy Plan," contains four consecutive steps, complete with supporting worksheets. The sidebars "IL in Action" and "IL in Action@URI" describes the actual planning process in our University of Rhode Island library and at other schools.

Step 1, "Plan to Plan," outlines the preliminary steps necessary to successfully create a comprehensive, effective, and practical document. This section covers how to establish a planning group, conduct needs assessment studies, gather background information, determine and adhere to timelines, select topics for coverage, and set up the writing team. We also provide a section (Section 1.7 Use Tips and Advice) accumulated from our experience.

Step 2, "Plan to Write," prepares the writing group for its task. It gives practical advice on the best ways to outline a structure for the plan, create a priority list, identify audiences, and launch a timetable for completion.

Step 3, "Write the Plan," discusses the key points of the document and the best methods for organizing content. It helps determine an appropriate timetable for completion and suggests the best methods for establishing an approval process. This section covers both content and layout.

Step 4, "Assess, Maintain, and Promote the Plan," emphasizes the ongoing and vital nature of a comprehensive information literacy plan. How do you care for, review, and revise it on a regular basis? How do you launch a marketing effort? What methods of assessment may be used? How do you measure and report progress?

Part II, "The Information Literacy (IL) Comprehensive Planning Toolkit," provides the support material to pull everything together. It includes several bibliographies on needs assessment literature, statistical data, an overview of information literacy to use in plan presentations to novices, success stories, and marketing materials.

Part III, "Model Real World IL Plans," features samples of successful information literacy plans—from a variety of colleges and universities across the country—to use as models or springboards for your own plan. The final resource is a list of hyperlinked addresses of model IL plans for use by various age-level students as they prepare for their college careers.

WHAT IS ON THE CD-ROM?

Creating a Comprehensive Information Literacy Plan features a companion CD-ROM that compiles the worksheets and other useful material from the guide. This feature allows institutions to reproduce and customize the worksheets. Readers can have one complete IL plan with step-by-step instructions.

This work is based on a simple but far-reaching idea: a good plan helps to ensure success with most endeavors. As information literacy expands from instruction at the point of need to a core mission of your library, we hope this guide will help you clarify your goals and streamline the process of realizing this most valuable ambition for your institution and the students it serves.

ACKNOWLEDGMENTS

We would like to acknowledge the assistance of the University of Rhode Island and the various librarians, teachers, administrators, and practitioners who provided examples of their experiences, especially Carol Ansel, Holly Barton, Jane Bradford, Carol Hansen, Kathleen McBroom, Kim Ranger, and Ross LaBaugh.

We would also like to thank all of the workshop participants who provided feedback.

And a special thank you to the following institutions for allowing us to reprint their information literacy plans:

Pine Point School
Stonington, Connecticut

Austin Community College Library
Austin, Texas

Vogel Library, Wartburg College
Waverley, Iowa

Roger Williams University Libraries
Bristol, Rhode Island

University of California Libraries
Los Angeles, California

Stewart Library, Weber State University
Ogden, Utah

1 CREATING A COMPREHENSIVE INFORMATION LITERACY PLAN

PLAN TO PLAN

INTRODUCTION

Before you write the first word of an information literacy document, you need to consider who, when, where, and how the planning process will happen. Do not think about the plan itself just yet. Think about the players, the timing, the surroundings in which you will meet, and what you want to accomplish. Think about the situation at your institution, the written and unwritten rules, and the chain of command. Look at the organization of your own institution and find out how it works. Every institution is different. Who belongs to what department, division, or college? Who supervises each segment? What is the reporting structure? Who can present a new program for approval? To whom is it submitted? How long will it take to get approval? What committees have to agree? Does the approval process go outside the institution? How are programs marketed on campus? What is said about programs in your course catalog? Can you "own" the program, or will you need to partner with someone else? When are the busy and slow times in your institution's calendar? Do you have a group of peer institutions? If not, get on the Web and find out what other institutions of your size and kind are doing. What information has been in the literature? Are there conferences or meetings you can attend to get information? In this section, we will discuss ideas about who, when, where, and how the planning process will happen.

1.1 ESTABLISH A PLANNING GROUP

No matter how large or small, complex or straightforward your institution's organization, deciding who to invite to the planning table is important. This initial stage is where you can attract and develop serious interest in your long-term goal from various audiences. Your choice of whom to invite to participate in the planning process is a strategic decision that will influence and propel support for your program within administrative, faculty, and student constituencies.

1.1.1 DECIDE WHO WILL DO THE PLANNING

Learn the organizational structure of your institution to help decide which audiences you might want to involve. Think broadly about any group that might provide support for the plan, from the president's office to athletics and recreation study hall advisors. In a school setting consider the Parent Teacher Organization or the Site Management Team. You will want to know who are the power players, change agents, and collaborators on your campus. If you do not have access to this information yourself, you should plan to meet and get to know the key people who will provide the inside scoop on groups such as the library board, the town or city school committee, the dean's council, the faculty senate and the student senate. Key players are often those people in middle management such as unit and team managers and support staff such as administrative assistants and secretaries. You will want to know who reports to whom, who supervises whom, and how change formally and informally happens on your campus.

If you can establish an ad hoc group for your library or school you may be able to handpick the members of the initial planning group. Be sure to do this strategically. Too large a group may make it difficult to gather a consensus of opinion that will impede progress; too small a group could create a situation where information gathering and reporting is delayed while members seek answers from outside the group. Include members from all or as many of the groups from which you want input and support: administrators, faculty, librarians, technologists, information specialists, support staff, instructional development specialists, and students. Regardless of how the planning group comes into existence, you will want to have a charge or a mission for your work. This will clarify and guide you as you investigate the possibilities for developing a plan for information literacy.

On the other hand, you may not be able to form your own group. The responsibility for planning may have been predetermined by your institution's established structure and its policies, rules, and regulations. If this is the case, you will need to find a way to present your ideas and a draft proposal within the preset structure. If you cannot physically meet with those responsible for planning, prepare a short overview of your ideas and provide it to the group or the group's leader. Try to gain a foothold in the established group and you may be invited to present the thumbnail sketch of your plan to develop a comprehensive information literacy plan. Ask people in the know if you may be appointed an ad hoc member during the time period that you expect to be developing the information literacy plan. This will be helpful in keeping the lines of communication open on both ends.

Membership in a planning committee will vary widely depending on your institutional rules and regulations. Use this worksheet to brainstorm about what kinds of people should be represented on your planning committee. Some suggestions are listed below. You will need to incorporate your knowledge of the local situation to include others who will be useful additions to your committee. Try to come up with all possibilities without regard to specific practical and/or political ramifications. You can always weed the list later.

Instructions: Brainstorm a possible list of candidates.

Librarians:

_____

_____

_____

_____

Friendly faculty:

_____

_____

_____

Administrators:

_____

_____

_____

School board/committee members:

_____

_____

_____

Students:

_____

_____

_____

Worksheet 1-A. Decide Who Will Do the Planning

IL in Action @ URI

The University Library at the University of Rhode Island is its own college; thus, we are self-governing. In 1998, our Dean convened a meeting of interested librarians to discuss developing an information literacy program. At subsequent meetings we invited various faculty members who were known to be active library supporters and already involved in our library instruction program.

IL in Action

Kathleen McBroom from the Dearborn, Michigan, public schools reported, "We had parental representation as well as teachers, administrators and media specialists (elementary, middle and high school levels)."

Holly Barton from Hope Valley Elementary School in Rhode Island, says that at her school she and the teachers were involved in the planning, but at the district level all of the library media specialists were involved in the planning process.

Carol Ansel from Pine Point School in Stonington, Connecticut, tells us that she was the planning committee for her school's plan.

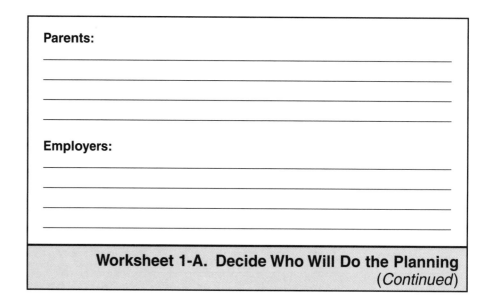

Parents:

Employers:

Worksheet 1-A. Decide Who Will Do the Planning
(Continued)

1.1.2 ESTABLISH WHEN YOUR GROUP WILL MEET

If you have been appointed to or joined an already established group, you might then become a member of an ad hoc committee or task force to investigate the ideas and plan the development and writing of the information literacy program. The group's first task will be to determine the best time to meet. If you have convened a group of your choosing you may have more latitude in deciding when the group will convene.

Keep in mind the possible times when the members of the planning group will be available. Refer to your institution's academic calendar and consider the timing of each planning group member's busy season. For example, if you plan a meeting during the first or last week of the school year, will you have good attendance and good attention? If you choose to meet during the winter intersession or spring break, will all the members be on campus? There may only be a few choices available based on the various duties and responsibilities of the members of your newly formed group. Offer the group some options that you feel will provide optimum work time to achieve your goal.

Think about a gathering of a large group of people. You must keep in mind not only your schedule but everyone else's schedule as well. In most educational institutions there is a rhythm and a cycle to the academic year. You should be able to determine times in the cycle when you will be likely to get the attendance and the input you want. Some suggestions are listed below. Brainstorm about the best times for your planning group to meet and jot them down.

Instructions: Brainstorm a list of possible meeting times.

Intersession (between semesters or trimesters):
_____
_____
_____
_____

Summer:
_____
_____
_____
_____

Year round (e.g., once a month, every other month):
_____
_____
_____
_____

In-service days:
_____
_____
_____
_____

Other times or intervals:
_____
_____
_____
_____

Worksheet 1-B. Establish When the Group Will Meet

IL in Action @ URI

At URI, we began our process with an open-space meeting. Four or five library staff members gathered at the assigned location for those interested in discussing teaching and learning. This group eventually became a task force charged with the mission of creating a program of library instruction that would meet the needs of all URI populations for the coming decade. The task force drafted the first of our thirteen versions of the Comprehensive Plan for Information Literacy at URI.

1.1.3 DECIDE ON THE FORMAT FOR THE MEETING(S) YOU WILL HAVE

Another task is to determine the format of the planning meetings that you will have. There are several meeting formats that encourage the free flow of ideas and brainstorming. Open-space meetings and retreats can provide a relaxed atmosphere that will stimulate ideas around the concepts of information literacy and its impact on the institution. Focus groups and task forces will have a set agenda and can determine the exact goals of information literacy for your institution.

Some institutions convene yearly open-space or common agenda events where all institution constituencies are invited to participate. At an open-space or common agenda meeting people sign up, show up, and participate in several days of sharing ideas and generally learning about each other's concerns and goals for the campus. At this type of meeting, you can generate excitement for your information literacy program ideas, as well as discover what other groups are doing that may overlap and support your goals. By learning what concerns other groups on campus have and perhaps collaborating with other programs, your group will establish more grassroots energy. This will be important at the approval stages for the information literacy plan.

A retreat can be a luxurious several-day stay at your institution's off-campus research center or a short and sweet one-day event on campus, away from e-mail, phones, and daily responsibilities. Retreats will be more focused than open-space meetings. You will need to plan the retreat ahead of time and develop activities that will allow participants to invest energy and encourage their creative forces. Generally, a comfortable atmosphere, good food, and fun activities will support a focused time period of serious thought on the information literacy goals that you want to discuss.

Ad hoc groups and task forces are more intense because of the short time frame and structured meeting styles in which they generally occur. These groups usually meet for a predetermined number of meetings over a set period of time. Members will be assigned particular tasks by the task force leader. A set timeline and method for reporting will be established with the hope of accomplishing a definite objective—establishing your information literacy plan.

Focus groups can be convened if you find the need to study the general response from the ideas generated at an open-space meeting or a retreat. Your group can make use of focus group activities to gather feedback on the proposed or draft ideas that you are considering. This may be useful at a large institution where there are many stakeholders to consider. The focus group approach also works for smaller institutions, where input from the group might provide necessary evidence to support the project's worthiness.

You may decide to have only one or many meetings. You may decide to try several different formats, with different groups of attendees at each. Brainstorm about the best way to get input from all the groups who will feel the impact of your plan.

Instructions: Brainstorm one or more formats for the meetings you will have.

Summer focus group:

_____
_____
_____
_____

Task force:

_____
_____
_____
_____

Retreat:

_____
_____
_____
_____

Open-space meeting:

_____
_____
_____
_____

Combine several of these options as appropriate:

_____
_____
_____
_____

Worksheet 1-C. Determine the Format(s) for the Meetings

1.2 CONDUCT A NEEDS ASSESSMENT STUDY

The planning group should conduct a needs assessment study to determine and establish the need for the information literacy plan. The goal of doing needs assessment is to provide a clear rationale for your information literacy plan and program. You will want to gather as complete and accurate a set of data as possible. Administrators may be very supportive of your idea to create a plan for information literacy at your institution, and, armed with assessment results as backup, they will be better able to address your requests for funding and staffing for the programs.

Needs assessment can be done using either passive or active methods. Determine which method will be more effective in your setting. Passive needs assessment can include casual assessments such as gathering anecdotal and observational evidence. Active needs assessment includes using focus groups, print or Web questionnaires, and oral surveys and interviews. You could consider developing different focus groups, one for each stakeholder population, and/or surveys or interviews for students, faculty, and librarians. Anyone who will be involved in the information literacy plan should be involved in order to gather as complete a picture as possible.

IL in Action @ URI

At URI, we used passive needs assessment methods. As reference librarians we knew the difficulties our students were having in finding, evaluating, and using information sources. As each year passed, and the number of databases increased and access to online sources improved, the requests from students for a course to "please teach us how to do this!" increased. We had direct contact with students and teachers at the reference desk and in the hundreds of library instruction sessions we provided. We were able to report anecdotal information to our superiors that reflected a need for an integrated multilevel information literacy program.

IL in Action

At Stetson University in Deland, Florida, librarian Jane Bradford reported that she created her document alone. She disseminated drafts to the other instruction librarians as needed. The final step was to have the entire library faculty review the plan before adopting it.

You will want to determine the best way to collect information about your institution's unmet needs for information literacy. We have listed some possible tools that could be used. Your decision about how best to collect information will be based on time, personnel, and available funding. Brainstorm as many possible information-gathering ideas as you can. Again, do not worry too much about the practicality of the ideas. Something that sounds crazy might just work!

Instructions: Brainstorm about methods you might use to collect data to show your institution's unmet needs.

Administer a student survey:

_____
_____
_____
_____

Collect anecdotal evidence:

_____
_____
_____
_____

Put a tally sheet at the reference desk and count the types of reference questions:

_____
_____
_____
_____

Ask questions on your faculty Listserv:

_____
_____
_____
_____

Do focus group interviews:

_____
_____
_____
_____

Worksheet 1-D. Explore Methods to Conduct a Needs Assessment

Observe library users doing research:

_____

_____

_____

_____

Give a quiz to randomly selected library users:

_____

_____

Worksheet 1-D. Explore Methods to Conduct a Needs Assessment (*Continued*)

1.3 GATHER BACKGROUND INFORMATION

In the planning group, look at the organizational charts for your institution and library. In order to gather useful background information you need to create the "big picture." Which groups have oversight over the long-term strategic plan for the institution? What have they done in the past and what are they hoping to accomplish over the short and long term? What accreditations are on the horizon for which colleges or departments? Which faculty or curriculum committees are concerned with and working toward student improvement of learning and outcomes assessment? What is the history, past and recent, of these groups? This is all part of developing your institutional knowledge, important in winning support for your information literacy plan. Once you have a sense of the "big picture," you can begin to see where parts of your plan might fit into it.

You may have members of your group who can contribute institutional knowledge. These are usually longtime faculty members, administrators, and support staff. Other places to gather background information about your campus are from the institution's college catalog of courses, student newspapers, alumni publications, foundation publications, minutes of meetings, annual reports, the university manual or other manuals of policies, procedures, and records. For elementary and secondary schools, also consult local, county, and statewide Department of Education reports.

1.3.1 EDUCATE THE PLANNING GROUP

Once the needs assessment project is in place, ask other group members to investigate the state, regional, and national information literacy scene. This will be particularly beneficial for those group members who are not as familiar or as knowledgeable about information literacy as you are. The more information you can share as a group the more committed the group will be to the same final recommendations and goals.

Assign one or two committee members to do a literature review on information literacy for peer institutions. They can summarize and report to the planning group what they have discovered. Direct the planning group members to read the ALA, ACRL, AASL Information Literacy web site pages. (See Step 3, page 62, 63 for a list of relevant Web addresses.) These Web site pages provide descriptions, standards, goals, objectives, and examples of information literacy and how it is being used in communities, K-12, and higher education. Arm your planning group with knowledge so that they can spread the word and educate their peers about the group's goals.

> **IL in Action**
>
> Peer Institutions
>
> Do you know who your peer institutions are? Ask your administrators for a list. Peer institutions are generally determined by criteria that include type of institution, size of student population, degrees offered, curriculums and programs offered, location, and/or funding levels. We have provided a bibliography of articles that discusses how to find your peer institutions in Part II, Step 5, section 5.3 of this book.

1.3.2 EDUCATE YOURSELF: READ THE LITERATURE

Broaden your knowledge of the information literacy plan possibilities for your campus by learning what other schools of the same size, type, or geographic location are doing with regard to information literacy.

As a librarian, you must read the professional literature on information literacy. Start a file that you can share with the committee, and perhaps ask members to read a few specific articles that provide possible program ideas for your institution. It is essential to be well-informed on the topic. Make it part of your group's work to keep up on the reading in as many journals as possible. If time is of the essence select a small number of journals and Web sites to read. You should also prepare an annotated bibliography to have on hand for future planning or writing groups. Bibliographies about information literacy are published annually in *Reference Services Review* and on the Library Instruction Round Table (LIRT) Web site, http://www3 .bayloc.edu/LIRT/. Other journals that feature articles about information literacy include *School Media Library Research, Knowledge Quest, College and Research Libraries, Reference Services Review, Reference and User Services, Reference Librarian, Journal of Academic Librarianship, Library Trends* (0024-2594), and *Research Strategies.*

1.3.3 ATTEND MEETINGS, WORKSHOPS, AND CONFERENCES

The planning group should take advantage of all available opportunities to attend meetings, workshops, and conferences that address student learning and information literacy. Look to local, regional, and national library and education groups to expand your knowledge base about information literacy planning and programming. The more information that you can gather the more prepared you will be to make quality decisions for your institution.

These groups offer annual conference programs and ongoing continuing education programs that often discuss information literacy. Become familiar with similar groups in your county, state, and region and then get involved with them. If you can, volunteer to help with conference or program planning for a specific group. In doing so, you may be able to help steer the direction of the conference or program offerings toward specific topics within information literacy about which your planning group needs to know.

In Rhode Island, for example, librarians are involved in the New England Library Association (NELA) and the Rhode Island Library Association (RILA). Both groups offer opportunities for learning more about information literacy through their various committees and annual programs. School media specialists belong to the Rhode Island Educational Media Association (RIEMA) and academic librarians belong to the ACRL New England Chapter (ACRL/NEC).

Nationally, there are several groups that offer information literacy workshops and conferences. The most well known are the ACRL Institute for Information Literacy's annual immersion program, the ACRL and ARL instruction section preconferences held at both the ALA midwinter and annual meetings, ACRL's biennial national conference, LOEX and Loex-of-the-West, and the Workshop on Instruction and Library Use (WILU) conference held annually in Canada.

Traveling to regional and national information literacy events does cost money that is often difficult to find in tight budgets. Consider signing up for an online course on topics related to information literacy. The Association of College and Research Libraries and the Association of Research Libraries sometimes offer courses that are about information literacy topics. You might consider signing up for an online credit course or continuing education program offered by a library and information studies program. When travel funds are severely limited, consider other options that will allow you to get firsthand information on existing information literacy plans.

1.3.4 GET ON THE WEB

Searching the Web is an obvious choice for free, flexible investigation of information literacy. There are many librarian-created Web sites devoted to information literacy. The following is a sampling of major information literacy Web sites:

ACRL Instruction Section
www.ala.org/ala/acrl/aboutacrl/acrlsections/instruction/homepage.htm

ACRL National Web Site's Information Literacy Pages
www.ala.org/ala/acrl/acrlissues/acrlinfolit/informationliteracy.htm

Big6: An Information Literacy Problem-Solving Process
www.big6.com/

Directory of Online Resources for Information Literacy (DORIL)
http://bulldogs.tlu.edu/mdibble/doril/

Institute for Information Literacy
www.ala.org/ala/acrl/acrlissues/acrlinfolit/professactivity/iil/welcome.htm

Library Instruction Round Table (LIRT)
www3.baylor.edu/LIRT/

LOEX Clearinghouse for Library Instruction
www.emich.edu/public/loex/loex.html

National Forum on Information Literacy
www.infolit.org

At all of these sites and at the Web sites of many libraries you will find an abundance of high-quality information on the various pieces of the information literacy plan you hope to create. If you hear about a program or plan that sounds appealing, use your Web-searching skills to ferret them out. Explore the information available online about each plan and program about which you are interested.

> **IL in Action @ URI**
>
> When we started searching for plans we used the same techniques that we teach our students: create the question, brainstorm keywords, use effective search techniques, evaluate the results, analyze the information, and apply the information appropriately. Take the time to learn to search for exactly what you need to find—in a sense, become information literate about information literacy.

1.3.5 COLD CALLING

Once you have identified programs of interest to you, e-mail or phone the person or persons in charge. Generally, most people are very willing to help out with suggestions or advice. Our experiences with cold calling have been very helpful. We learned about the highlights and pitfalls of many plans and programs by e-mailing or speaking with the people who actually created the documents and implemented the plans. After using our plan for information literacy at URI for four years we have been able to reciprocate by sharing our experiences as we answer librarians' e-mails and phone calls about our plan and by presenting our story at local, regional, and national conferences.

1.3.6 MAKE SITE VISITS

The best way to gather information and gain advice is to actually visit an institution that has implemented an information literacy plan. If you are within easy traveling distance, consider arranging a day-long site visit. You could interview the students, librarians, and faculty who are involved in the plan, visit a class or workshop, and see first hand the work that is being done at that institution. If the plan you have identified as a perfect fit is more than a day trip for your group, suggest that the group request funding to visit the institution to find out more. Nothing can compare with getting a bird's-eye view of the actual work site where the plan is in operation.

If you have funding to attend a national or regional conference, it might be possible to extend your stay and visit targeted sites with information literacy programs of interest to you. While this strategy will depend on the serendipity of the conference location and the sites you want to visit, if you have a geographic match this strategy will help you take advantage of travel funding you may already have and make it do double duty.

There are many ways to gather information about what other institutions are doing. It is important to know what others have tried and what worked for them. It's also good to know which ideas failed and why. Listed below are some ideas we have tried, but there are certainly others. Brainstorm and note down as many ideas as you can about how you can find out about what other institutions are doing with regard to information literacy.

Instructions: Brainstorm ideas about how you can find out what other institutions are doing about information literacy.

Read the literature:

_____
_____
_____
_____

Identify similar institutions:

_____
_____
_____
_____

Attend information literacy or other conferences:

_____
_____
_____
_____

Get on the Web:

_____
_____
_____
_____

Call/e-mail or otherwise contact colleagues:

_____
_____
_____
_____

Worksheet 1-E. List Ways to Gather Background Information

Make site visits as you are able:

_____

_____

_____

_____

**Worksheet 1-E. List Ways to Gather Background
Information** (*Continued*)

1.4 DETERMINE AND ADHERE TO TIMELINES

Your planning group will need to know how much time to allow for investigating each topic of interest and when to move toward the next steps in developing the plan for information literacy. In order to do this, create a projected timeline for your project. Commit to writing the meeting minutes and scheduled information-gathering reports on a timely basis. Decide at the beginning how often you will report and which other groups will receive your minutes and reports. Be sure to post all of your public minutes and reports on a planning group Listserv, on the project's Web site, in the library's newsletter and Web site, and anywhere else where they can be read.

If your planning group is made up of people who are representatives of other campus stakeholder groups be sure to have those members report to their larger groups on a regular basis. If you are not part of a larger group arrange to keep those other groups informed. Getting the word out on your planning progress will insure that important information travels throughout your institution, through the ranks, and up the chain of command. Develop important administrative commitment by meeting with or reporting to larger groups such as a council of deans or faculty senate group.

In order to finish any large project time limits must be imposed. Setting deadlines will motivate committee members to do their homework and will define how long you will spend on each topic. As each phase is completed, you will want to put your findings in writing so that you can go back to them and show your progress. Below are some examples of the kinds of things you may want to put into your timetable. Brainstorm ideas about how long the investigation and information-gathering phase of each part of your plan should take. (*Hint*: It may be easier to set a completion date and work backwards!) Also, brainstorm about how and to whom you want (or must) report your progress.

Instructions: Brainstorm about how long it will take to create or accomplish your entire plan. Determine how often you will report to the people overseeing the process.

Complete an outline for a comprehensive plan that will go to library faculty and university administration for approval:

_____

_____

_____

_____

Needs assessment progress report to planning committee:

_____

_____

_____

_____

Focus group or open-space meetings progress report to planning committee:

_____

_____

_____

_____

Background information-gathering progress report to planning committee:

_____

_____

_____

_____

Worksheet 1-F. Agree on Timelines and Report Results

Topic selection progress report to library director:

_____

_____

_____

_____

Create a writing group and submit a list of appointees to library director:

_____

_____

_____

_____

Send progress reports to library director, faculty, administration, school board, and so on:

_____

_____

_____

_____

Worksheet 1-F. Agree on Timelines and Report Results
(_Continued_)

1.5 SELECT TOPICS AND DECIDE WHAT TO ACCOMPLISH

The planning committee has now set up a dependable framework for creating an information literacy plan. Your planning group has a clear vision of when, where, how, and why they are meeting. The group is armed with a rich and varied background on the information literacy field. The real work has begun! Now you must engage in studying, selecting, and eventually weeding through the information that you have gathered to cull those parts of plans and programs that will work together to serve your particular institution.

During the information-gathering phase, the planning committee should examine a wide variety of information literacy plans and programs. Each will offer an array of information literacy instructional opportunities, some offered by the library and others offered institutionwide by both librarians and instructional technology personnel. Make note of the different content, various delivery methods, levels of intensity, and short- and long-term goals of each plan and program. You will find dozens of online information literacy tutorials, some interactive, others simply pages of instruction for students to read. There are required and optional seminars, drop-in and mandatory workshops, credit-bearing courses, and much information literacy instruction delivered via integrated, course-related, and "one-shot" library instruction sessions. You will find institutions that use the "train the trainer" approach, those that teach individual faculty how to implement information literacy in their courses, and those that deliver information literacy concepts and skills directly from the library to the students on their campus. What will work for your institution? What will your administrators invest in? That is the challenge faced by the planning group.

We recommend using the ACRL Best Practices Initiative document, "Characteristics of Programs of Information Literacy That Illustrate Best Practices: A Guideline," found at www.ala.org/ala/acrl/acrlstandards/characteristics.htm as a guide to determine the areas that should be included in the planning document that you create. The following areas are fully articulated in this document: mission statement, goals, objectives, planning, administrative and institution support, articulation with the curriculum, collaboration, pedagogy, staffing, outreach, and assessment/evaluation. Each area should be given considerable attention and investigation. A well-designed and implemented plan for information literacy should work like a well-oiled engine with all parts working together to propel and support student learning at your institution.

Do not work in a vacuum when creating the mission statement, goals, and objectives of your information literacy plan. Consult your institution's mission statement for ideas on how and where your proposed ideas will mesh with the larger scope of the institution. Does your library have its own mission statement? You may find that your ideas help support concepts already embedded in the broader mission of both the library and the institution.

Consider the goals of the major programs on your campus. Is there a college or program looking to increase students' critical thinking, use of information technology, and research concepts and skills? Is your state's Department of Education mandated to achieve student learning standards? How are they working toward this goal? Your plan could be a welcome addition in support of an already-established college or program's goals by including these wider institution goals and objectives in the plan for information literacy. Review major programs of study at various levels. Find out what level of research skill is expected of students at various points in their studies. Are there distinct institutionwide patterns for research skill competencies? Looking at all of these areas will help your group begin defining the mission, goals, and objectives for the information literacy plan.

While meeting with various groups you will gather many ideas about what could be put in your plan. At some point, you will have to decide what you will include and which ideas have to be set aside. You should try to be as comprehensive as possible and use your imagination so that your programs can expand within the confines of your plan.

Instructions: Brainstorm about topics you might include when shaping your plan.

Administration and institutional support:

_____

_____

_____

_____

Articulation with curriculum:

_____

_____

_____

_____

Pedagogy:

_____

_____

_____

_____

Staffing:

_____

_____

_____

_____

Outreach:

_____

_____

_____

_____

Assessment:

_____

_____

_____

Worksheet 1-G. Select Topics to Include in the Plan

_____

_____

Space:

_____

_____

_____

_____

Budget:

_____

_____

Worksheet 1-G. Select Topics to Include in the Plan
(*Continued*)

1.5.1 ADMINISTRATION AND INSTITUTIONAL SUPPORT

This area can be a wrestling match for many institutions. Most administrators will agree that creating an information literacy plan and program is a good idea, a positive thing, an important goal for the library. Grappling with budgets to find the staffing and funding to support the plan and program is the quest that stymies many would-be information literacy programs. In this arena, be skillful! Look at what you do now that can be retooled to support the program. Look at budgets to see where funding is already available for some of your goals. Identify possible start-up funds from campus, local, regional, and national grant agencies. Institutions need to continually support the information literacy staff by funding professional development and continuing education opportunities.

1.5.2 ARTICULATION WITH THE CURRICULUM

If your planning group includes members from a variety of campus constituencies, you will have already achieved a modicum of articulation with the curriculum. Members will contribute valuable information about how their field of study will benefit from the addition of information literacy goals. They also will relay reports to their departments and spread the good word about the work that you are doing. Continue to reach out across the campus to as many stakeholder groups, departments, and programs as possible as you develop the plan for information literacy. Your goal should be to have it be as inclusive as possible by reaching out to as many varied departments and programs as you can. At the same time, do not be daunted by

IL in Action @ URI

At URI, we introduced our first credit-bearing course in spring 1998. No additional staffing or funding were provided. As semesters have progressed, we have been able to get additional reference desk positions to cover the time librarians would have been working on the reference desk. These positions have been funded based on student credit hours from our LIB120 course. Other staffing is provided by URI-GSLIS students who either work for the Reference Unit or participate in Professional Field Experience credit projects for the Reference Unit.

the limited number of groups who may sign on to the initial plan. As you develop the plan and implement the program, the strength of its reputation will attract others who will want to become involved.

1.5.3 PEDAGOGY

The area that requires particular research and attention is pedagogy. The planning group should investigate and be knowledgeable about learning theories, learning styles, and information literacy models. Current pedagogical practice tends to advocate student-centered learning, which makes use of resource-based learning, problem-based learning, and active learning methods. Consult the experts at your institution's Center for Teaching Excellence or Faculty Development Program for recommendations on the current thinking on your campus regarding learning theories and learning styles.

1.5.4 STAFFING

Providing staffing to implement the plan for information literacy need not be insurmountable. Whether you are developing the plan as a mandate from the higher-ups or from the grass roots, the need for staffing will be recognized by administration. If you are following a mandate it may be easier to secure the staffing you need. If you are creating your plan as a grassroots effort, the onus may be on the planning group to identify and find support for staffing.

Most librarians are already involved in delivering information literacy concepts and skills. You should assess the time involved in the already-established instruction program and retool and revamp each librarian's workload or daily schedule to reflect the goals of the new plan/program. Look at the ideas that you have developed in the areas of collaboration, articulation with the curriculum, and pedagogy. Which faculty and staff from outside of the library are involved in the development process? Will implementing the plan involve including librarians, graduate students, subject faculty, and first-year staff? Do not be afraid to use all available levels of staffing.

1.5.5 OUTREACH

The document "Characteristics of Programs of Information Literacy That Illustrate Best Practices: A Guideline" (Best Practices Initiative. Institute for Information Literacy. ACRL, June 2003, American Library Association) outlines several excellent suggestions for developing outreach opportunities. Consider developing formal and informal marketing plans.

IL in Action @ URI

At URI, we consulted our Instructional Development Program (IDP) for help with designing assignments and surveys for our LIB120 course. Most of the LIB120 instructors have attended annual weeklong IDP workshops. Later, two of our instructors became IDP Teaching Fellows for an academic yearlong program.

You could develop a campuswide newsletter devoted to the ongoing work of the planning group or write a column in a faculty or student publication. Perhaps a member of your group could contribute an occasional summary report for the campuswide faculty Listserv or news publication. Consult with the institution's news bureau, alumni relations group, or public relations team to develop a press release or even a feature article on the big plans you are developing. The feature piece could be distributed to local and state newspapers. If you use the model illustrated in the following sidebar, you could speak with the local or campus radio station and develop a series of public service announcements that promulgate various aspects of your plan, or you could discuss one information literacy concept on a weekly basis.

IL in Action

Ross LaBaugh, coordinator of library instruction at California State University–Fresno developed a series of radio features called *InfoRadio*. These radio spots feature actual research tools and ideas and provide information literacy instruction right in the radio spot. Your radio spots could advertise your services, announce your new information literacy plan, or follow the *InfoRadio* model that CSU has provided:

InfoRadio is a series of radio features designed to teach information competency skills to college and university students. Similar to National Public Radio information programs like *A Moment in Time* and *Star Date*, *InfoRadio* spots are about two minutes long and focus on a specific reference tool, Web site, or research skill. Airing on the CSU–Fresno campus radio station, *InfoRadio* features are available to libraries throughout the CSU system, and libraries outside the CSU system can purchase the series.

More information about *InfoRadio*, including transcripts and audio samples, are available on the *InfoRadio* Web site, www.csuinforadio.org (Accessed: 19 July 2005).

1.5.6 ASSESSMENT AND EVALUATION

Assessment and evaluation should be ongoing and address all of the following issues: program performance as a whole; course, workshop, or seminar evaluations; one-shot library-instruction-session evaluations; student learning outcomes; and instructor teaching evaluations. Finding the time to complete assessments and evaluations is not always easy but it is necessary. The literature and the Web are teeming with information on how to assess and evaluate information literacy. There is much to know about assessment and evaluation that we cannot adequately cover here. We will offer some ideas and point out major concepts and projects in Section 4.2. For more information on how to implement assessment and evaluation, please see our brief bibliography at the end of section 4.2.

As we leave this section, remember that the group that actually implements your institution's information literacy plan can refer to this list again in the assessment phase of the plan.

1.6 CREATE WRITING GROUP

When it comes to planning to write the information literacy plan, you may want to consider having a small group of three do the writing. It will be easier to juggle schedules and craft a document with a single voice if the writing group is small. This group can draft parts of the plan and send them on to a larger group for comments, additions, deletions, and editorial work. Most large groups find it easier to have something in writing to react to, rather than trying to create an original document. On the other hand, you might want specific groups to write about their own areas; for example, faculty might write about credit-bearing courses, instruction librarians about library instruction, and the Webmaster could write about online tutorials and user guides.

The first thing you will want to determine is the composition of your writing group. Again, this will depend on individual situations: You alone may have the task of drafting the plan, a standing committee may be asked to do it, or an administrator may select individuals to work together to draft the plan. The rules of your institution may require certain people to be members of your writing team. The important thing to remember is that you want to have at least one member of the group who writes well, knows the mechanics of the writing process, and who speaks the language of your institution.

If you are the decision maker, whom would you choose, and who might you be allowed to choose? Are you required to have certain people on your committee? Do you have the authority to create a writing group with members of your choosing? Find out what authority you have and then plan accordingly.

Here are some possibilities for the makeup of a writing team:

Librarians

You might have all librarians on your writing task force. If the program is going to reside in the library and the librarians are going to be the instructors, they will be closest to the subject and have the most insight into the problems and advantages of the day-to-day operation of the plan.

IL in Action @ URI

At the University of Rhode Island, a small committee of library faculty met to put into words what options might be available to us for developing an information literacy program, what were the needs of our students and faculty, and how information literacy could be delivered to all interested parties. We felt that the library faculty was the best-informed group overall on campus with respect to information literacy, library services, facilities, personnel, and the information literacy needs of the students. As the bulk of the work of creating the plan would fall to library personnel, who could better craft such a plan? As faculty members it fell within our purview to create and sponsor a program of information literacy for the university.

The writing team did not work in a vacuum. The drafts prepared by the library committee were sent as written reports to the larger Public Services Department for discussion, review, and revision. Once approved, the draft information literacy plan was sent to the Library Curriculum Committee for review. In this manner, the revision and approval processes continued.

Faculty

You may want (or be required) to include faculty from outside the library on your writing team. They may offer a different classroom perspective or work with a segment of the student population you do not see very often. They will have good ideas about how information literacy could be incorporated into their curriculum. You might even find someone who has written a successful plan for another campus program! Try to make maximum use of the talent and experience in your own backyard.

Administrators

Administrators will be admirably prepared to provide your plan with the phrases and style most favored on your campus. They are usually practiced in the fine art of writing plans and proposals and can be of great benefit to a writing team. They also can be helpful in getting the attention and cooperation of those whose approval you may need.

An administrator who is part of the writing committee or task force can be especially useful if the individual is also part of the chain of command that approves the document. The details of funding, personnel, and equipment may be more available to an administrator who can bring that perspective to the table.

Committees

You know the old joke about a camel being the end result of a committee trying to design a horse? Sometimes committees are not the best vehicle for accomplishing a complex task. On the other hand, with the right combination of committee members, much can be accomplished through each person's experience and viewpoint. It may be possible to divide the work of writing among several individuals or groups if they are carefully chosen.

IL in Action

In a school setting, classroom instructors are involved in assigning the students' projects. At Pine Point School, Stonington, Connecticut, Carol Ansel states, "I get constant input/feedback from classroom teachers and try to dovetail with their classroom research needs." Faculty membership on the writing team can help incorporate the classroom perspective and bring to light the realities of project-based learning that may not be evident to others.

IL in Action @ URI

At URI, we began with a small writing group of three people. We drafted ideas that were presented to our slightly larger task force. In the task force meetings we revised, edited, and added to the document in hand. This interplay continued until we had a "complete" draft that was presented to larger groups, up the chain of command. At each larger meeting suggestions were noted in detail. We then went back and revised, sending the new document up the chain again. We found that a smaller group creating a proposal was something that larger groups could react to in an efficient and effective manner.

IL in Action

Kathleen McBroom from the Dearborn, Michigan, public schools reports that "[A] committee of approximately ten people met for fifteen full-day sessions during the school year over the three year period."

Carol Ansel of Pine Point School in Stonington, Connecticut, states that "When I started the job seventeen years ago, I inherited nothing. I worked my way through things week by week that first year, then have continually 'tweaked' and modified my curriculum ever since. Guess you might say it's never finished."

Writing the document calls for a smaller group. You will probably want to have practitioners—those who will deliver some part of the program—in the group. You will also want to select the best writers you can. If you were allowed to choose anyone you wanted to be part of your writing group, who would it be? We have listed some categories below. Knowledge of your particular situation will probably provide you with additional ideas. Brainstorm about who will be the best wordsmith of your document. Again, make your list as broad and as wishful as you want.

Instructions: Brainstorm about who will do the writing of your plan.

Librarians:

_____

_____

_____

_____

Faculty:

_____

_____

_____

_____

Administrators:

_____

_____

_____

_____

Existing writing committees:

_____

_____

_____

_____

Professional writers:

_____

_____

_____

_____

Worksheet 1-H. Choose Who Will Write the Plan

1.7 USE TIPS AND ADVICE

Following, you will find some general advice that we gathered as we went through the process of creating a comprehensive plan for information literacy at our institution.

1.7.1 BE AS CLEAR AND AS DETAILED AS POSSIBLE

When setting out the contents of your plan for information literacy, be as clear and as detailed as possible in describing the various parts of your plan. Lay it out so that it is both easy to read and visualize. Explain where each segment and each option fits in to the students' program of study. Discuss what students will learn in each segment, and how their learning will be assessed.

1.7.2 PROVIDE OPTIONS

Provide students with as many delivery options as possible. Be as flexible and as inclusive as you can. Methods for achieving competencies may include: in-class exercises, homework assignments, papers, projects, on-line/offline work, courses, workshops, Web tutorials. Build on what you already do and call on local experts to help you expand from that base. Suggest areas in your institution's curriculum (courses, programs, special projects) where pieces of your information literacy plan might be useful.

1.7.3 THINK INCREMENTAL AND MODULAR

Make your offerings incremental and modular. This will allow implementation of your plan one piece at a time. While it is wonderful to think about dropping an entire plan into place and making all parts of it run at a selected point in time, it may be necessary and perhaps even desirable to introduce parts of your information literacy plan separately over a period of time. In practical matters such as personnel, funding, and space, implementing your plan incrementally may be the only way to make the entire plan a reality.

1.7.4 LINK YOUR PLAN TO NATIONAL COMPETENCIES

Link exercises, tutorials, and activities in each piece of your plan to the ACRL Competencies, the AASL Competencies, or other approved and

---

IL in Action @ URI

At our presentation to the council of deans, we suggested that our three-credit course would fit well in the Learning Communities for freshmen offered during the fall semester each year. Learning communities consist of groups of freshmen who take a group of classes together as a community or cohort. Classes for the communities usually consist of some combination of general course work that will mesh as far as skills and subject matter are concerned. Our three-credit course, "Introduction to Information Literacy" works well with any class requiring research and/or term-paper-level writing assignments. The council of deans agreed that this would be a good fit.

IL in Action @ URI

At URI, we had a limited number of people available to work on this project and had to address the implementation of our plan one step at a time. We opted to work on our credit courses first. We also had a technology-savvy, graduate library school student looking for field experience. To accommodate his needs with the needs outlined in our plan we worked together to create our online tutorial. If our plan had been too rigid we might not have been able to accomplish this portion of the plan.

recognized professional groups whose competencies are appropriate for your institution. Be sure to state which competencies are addressed in each part of the plan.

1.7.5 VARY YOUR TEACHING METHODS

Use teaching methods to accommodate multiple intelligences. In creating your classes, tutorials, modules, and exercises try to balance what students like to do with what they need to know. Students enjoy learning information literacy through active learning techniques. Design the delivery of your program using active learning, resource-based learning, and/or problem-based learning. Keep in mind that people learn differently, some are visual learners, some are verbal learners, some are tactile learners. Try to provide enough variety in all parts of your plan so that all types of learners can benefit.

1.7.6 DEVELOP MEASURABLE OUTCOME TOOLS

Develop and include measurable assessment tools to measure outcomes for each segment and delivery option you plan to offer. Everyone you talk to will want to know how you know your program is successful. Assessment can take many forms including pre- and posttests, focus groups, surveys, opinion polls, student evaluations, and so on. Measures of whether students are achieving the competencies you have targeted will be necessary to "prove" the effectiveness of your program to both skeptics and believers.

1.7.7 DO NOT LIMIT YOUR PLAN TO STUDENTS

Build methods for educating faculty and administrators about information literacy into your plan. Encourage faculty to incorporate information literacy into their curriculum and to send students to your classes and/or tutorials so that they become proficient in the world of research and how it has changed during the past ten years. You may want to build tutorials, exercises, bibliographies, and other tools specifically for faculty, or you may want to offer to faculty what you have already created for students. You may also want to provide exclusive and intensive workshop sessions for faculty. Ask to be part of new faculty orientations and work to create new avenues for reaching the nonstudents on campus.

1.7.8 THINK BIG, START SMALL, BUT BEGIN!

Take your opportunities as they come. Everything may not fall into place at one time. You may have to choose one small project and stick with it. You

IL in Action

Carol Hansen of Weber State University in Ogden, Utah, reports, "Every fall a retreat for new faculty hires is held at a mountain resort. A librarian is always at the retreat to network with new faculty and present an orientation session on information literacy. This is a very useful opportunity for continually growing partnerships and influencing attitudes of new faculty towards IL at WSU."

may have to implement pieces of the plan earlier than anticipated or in a different order. You may be presented with multiple opportunities in the same semester. Be flexible so you can take advantage of opportunities as they come along.

On the other hand, do not promise more than you can deliver. You may get requests for multiple parts of your plan to be implemented at the same time. Be thoughtful and strategic in deciding which opportunities to choose. Be sure to state why you cannot accommodate the requests that you turn down, or, better yet, give a target date for when you might be able to address specific requests if you cannot work on them immediately.

STEP 2 PLAN TO WRITE

2.1 MEET AND DISCUSS WRITING STRATEGIES

Once your writing group members have been named, one of the first things the group will need to do is meet to discuss writing strategies. They must be clear about which goals have been identified for the information literacy plan. They must decide how to go about creating the document that will outline and detail the plan. Meeting times, writing assignments, electronic sharing of drafts, and the order in which the plan will be written are all aspects of the writing strategy to consider.

2.1.1 DISCUSS GOALS

Be sure you have a clear idea of what you want your plan to accomplish as you get started. Presumably, you will have decided something about the goals and objectives you have in mind during your planning sessions. Those goals and objectives should be guiding principals for the writing group and should be distributed to each member of the group before the writing begins. Below you will find some possible goals to think about.

Provide a Blueprint for Information Literacy

Your institution may want to create a road map that will guide the institution as it creates an information literacy program. This blueprint will provide instructions about how the whole program works, even if every person working in the library today retired tomorrow.

Give the Library More Publicity/Status on Campus

It never hurts to provide the library with a new source of positive publicity. You could make publicity for the library as one goal in your plan. You may

IL in Action @ URI

One very common complaint in academic libraries is that faculty and administrators do not seem to know what services are offered at the library. At URI, one of our goals in writing the information literacy plan was to have an official document that we could use to inform and educate the rest of the campus community about teaching in the library.

IL in Action @ URI

At URI, we had a long-term vision about what we wanted information literacy to look like in ten years. We created a plan that would take us to that goal one step at a time. As it turned out, we became so involved in launching and teaching our three-credit course that, several years later, we really needed to refer to the plan to find out what to do next.

want to provide a document to inform readers that library personnel are very much involved in the teaching mission of their institutions. This may be a new concept for some of your potential readers.

Provide Information for All Interested Parties

Administrators frequently request reports from colleges or departments about new or innovative programs that can be used as talking points at those very important budget meetings and fund-raising events. A goal for your document might be to provide administrators with the details that will make your program one of the things they talk about.

Keep the Institutional Community Up to Date

University personnel outside the library do not necessarily keep up with what is going on in the world of libraries and what librarians do within those hallowed halls. One goal for your plan might be to make everyone aware of new services in the library that could improve the lives of students, faculty, and administrators alike.

Make a Guide to Get Your Information Literacy Program to Its Completed Form

One goal might be to have a document that would help keep your progress focused and get you back on track if you get bogged down along the way. It may take some time to get parts of your plan operational, and you may have to concentrate time and energy on one part of the plan before you can move on to the next. One goal for your plan might be to have it serve as a step-by-step guide to the finished program.

Think about what you actually want your written document to accomplish. You may have any number of goals in mind. It will be useful to articulate those goals, as they will inform the contents and the length of the document. Below is a short list of possible goals.

Instructions: Brainstorm about the goals you would like to achieve with the written plan.

Provide a blueprint for information literacy at my institution:

_____
_____
_____
_____

Give the library more publicity/status on campus:

_____
_____
_____
_____

Create an informational tool for all interested parties:

_____
_____
_____
_____

Keep the institutional community up-to-date:

_____
_____
_____
_____

Create a manual for completing your information literacy program:

_____
_____
_____
_____

Worksheet 2-A. Clarify the Goals You Want to Accomplish with the Plan

IL in Action @ URI

In the plan at URI, we created a tiered system of instruction that is delivered to students at various points throughout their college careers. We decided that the best way to convey this information was to create a chart (see www.uri.edu/library/instruction_services/infolitplan.html) that shows what information will be delivered to freshmen, sophomores, juniors, and seniors. The chart also includes plans for delivering instruction to instructors, faculty, teaching assistants, and other teaching personnel.

2.2 OUTLINE A STRUCTURE FOR THE PLAN

Think about how to put your goals and objectives into a document that makes sense. You might list the first goal/objective and describe it in detail, then move on. You might list all goals and objectives and then go back to explain each in turn. You might want to break your goals and objectives into categories or groups of like ideas and write about each in turn. You might want to align your goals and objectives with a document like the ACRL Information Literacy Competencies so it is easy to see how your plan lines up with the national standards.

Think about the form(s) your plan could take. In that you will want to have a document that covers all the nuts and bolts of the process, you will have to decide how best to present the plan on paper. You may be able to give your plan a shape before you begin writing. Create an outline or a sketch of what you want your plan to look like.

Look at the ACRL Information Literacy Competencies. This document can provide guidance as it lists the information literacy goals point by point. You will want to determine where in your plan you hope to address each of your identified goals. The competencies are the backbone of information literacy in U.S. academic libraries. The AASL also provides approved standards for school libraries, and some professions have specified competencies as well. (See Step 3, Information Literacy Standards and Competencies.)

The structure of your document is important as it will make the job of reading and understanding your plan easy or hard. In Step 3 we give some examples of plans for information literacy. Make it part of the planning work of your writing group(s) to look at plans others have devised and learn from what they have done. You may find some ideas you had not thought about before. Seeing the layout and organization of someone else's plan will help you to structure your own.

Your plan will have many parts that will amount to a complex whole, but try to keep it as simple as you can, even if there are multiple facets to it. Plan to use language everyone can understand, even if they are not well versed in the language of your institution.

2.3 CREATE A WRITING PRIORITY LIST

The best starting point will depend on your individual situation. In some instances it might make sense to start with the content itself—what content will be delivered to what audience at what time—and work backwards from there. In other cases, the starting point might address the most obvious needs that surfaced from the needs assessment you did. If you are the information literacy designee for your institution, you might select a starting point based on whom you can convince to help you. You might want to write a history of your library instruction program to date. You may want to look at documents that already exist, such as the mission statement and goals for your institution and your library. Some writing that is appropriate to your document may already have been created for another document. Following is a list of parts of the plan you might want to address. Think about making and ranking your list so you know what topics you will address and in what order.

Introduction and Justification

Every plan needs something that will explain to the reader why it is being written, what it is proposing, and why it is important. Your writing group may feel that this section of the document is the most important as it will help focus the rest of the writing. The writing group(s) can refer to it for guidance once it is completed. Perhaps you will decide to work on this part first.

Identify and Prepare Instructors

Identification of those people who will deliver your program will be of interest to the teachers themselves, to those who supervise them, and to the administrators who have to pay them. Preparation is necessary before the program can be delivered to students. Will teachers need major and lengthy training or will a one-day workshop suffice? Writing this part of the plan early may be key to the success of other parts of the plan.

Ideas about New Credit Courses

If you hope to include for-credit courses in your information literacy plan, the content needs to be thought out and documented early in the process. If you already offer a course or have a program of library instruction, information about them should be spelled out, if it has not already been done. If

IL in Action @ URI

At URI, we thought out and planned both our one-credit and three-credit courses as we wrote our comprehensive plan. We were able to include the documentation we used to get our courses approved in our plan. Although this required a lot of work and concentrated effort for several months, the result was that both courses were approved and both were incorporated into the plan.

it has been written, using your existing document may be an easy way to give your writing group a place to start.

Partnering with Faculty

You may already have some relationships with classroom faculty and work collaboratively with them. Plans for how this will continue, expand, or change will be useful to everyone. Or you may have some new ideas or mandates from the administration about library-classroom partnerships. Getting this information into writing and getting the approval from the teachers involved may be a high priority for you.

Undergraduates versus Graduate Students

Which segment of your student population needs instruction in information literacy the most? Is there a mechanism that can be easily used to reach your first target population? The University of Rhode Island requires all students to take URI 101: Traditions and Transformations: a Freshman Seminar. This is a one-credit course intended to acquaint new students with college life in general, and with college life at URI in particular. Undergraduates are also required to fulfill General Education requirements. Making our three-credit course an option in the General Education English Communications requirement gave us entrée to a large number of undergraduates as well. In our view, then, it made sense to write the part of the plan that dealt with the undergraduate population before we wrote about graduate students.

Subject-specific Instruction

Perhaps faculty members have contacted you for assistance in teaching research methods in their subject-area classes. It might be beneficial to craft this part of the plan early on in order to capitalize on such an opportunity.

IL in Action @URI

At URI, Mary and Andrée were contacted by a professor at the Business School who wanted all students who declared a business major to have information literacy training along with one of their required courses. By working with this faculty member, a one-credit "lab" was created that taught information literacy concepts and skills with an emphasis on business resources. This lab has become LIB 140 and can be adapted to any subject area.

Refer back to your Worksheet 1-G. This is where you identified all the items you wanted to include in your plan. The parts of the plan don't necessarily have to be written in the order in which they appear in the document. You may want to schedule the writing of parts of the plan based on documents that already exist, information already at hand and partnerships that have already been established. This will help to get parts of the plan written quickly and help to give the plan shape and substance right away. Prioritize the list created in Worksheet 1-G to identify in what order you intend to write the sections. You may also wish to identify the individual and/or group who will be responsible for producing the section and the deadline anticipated.

Instructions: Brainstorm about how you might want to prioritize different parts of your plan.

Priority #1:

Topic: _____

Writer: _____

Deadline: _____

Priority #2:

Topic: _____

Writer: _____

Deadline: _____

Priority #3:

Topic: _____

Writer: _____

Deadline: _____

Priority #4:

Topic: _____

Writer: _____

Deadline: _____

Priority #5:

Topic: _____

Writer: _____

Deadline: _____

Worksheet 2-B. Prioritize Topics to Include in the Plan

Priority #6:

Topic: _____

Writer: _____

Deadline: _____

Priority #7:

Topic: _____

Writer: _____

Deadline: _____

Priority #8:

Topic: _____

Writer: _____

Deadline: _____

Worksheet 2-B. Prioritize Topics to Include in the Plan
(*Continued*)

2.4 IDENTIFY YOUR AUDIENCE

You are putting your plan into writing so that someone will read it. Who do you want to read it? Is there one key group or person you want to reach, or is your document meant to be useful to a wider or more diverse group? Will you need to write more than one document, or different versions, to accommodate the needs of your various readers? In the planning stage, you will want to know the intended audience and what they want/need to know about your information literacy plan. Once you have resolved these issues, you will have a better idea of how long the writing process might take.

2.4.1 DETERMINE AUDIENCE(S) FOR THE PLAN

There are many different groups associated with your institution that have an interest in information literacy. Think broadly in order to include as wide an audience as possible for your plan. Knowing your audience will make it easier to craft a document using language that your audience will understand. If you want to reach a number of groups (both students and administrators, for example), you might think about creating different versions of the plan for each audience. Students will want to know how the plan is going to help them get their degrees and get jobs. Administrators will want to know how it is going to strengthen the reputation of the institution and what it is going to cost. Your writing group will want to think about how you can provide the information that both students and administrators need.

The following list includes some audiences you might want to consider when you begin to write your plan. Leave open the possibility that you may have to write more than one version of your plan to highlight the segments of most interest to each audience.

Institutional Administration

The administration might use your plan as a selling point for the institution. They will want to be able to access every detail. Administrators, however, are busy people, and they also will be happy to have an executive summary that outlines and highlights what is important to them, but does not dwell on the details. They will also want to have some idea of the costs involved in the implementation of your plan. In short, they will want both the big picture and the details of your plan available to them.

Library Administration

Library administration will want to know all the details, from soup to nuts. They will want to have all questions addressed, from personnel to paperclips. They will need to have the answers when the higher-ups call.

Faculty

Faculty will want to know how this plan will change their lives. Will it make their jobs easier or harder? Will they have more work to do or less? Details of expected positive outcomes and how they apply to other classroom settings will be important information for faculty.

Students

Students might not be the group most likely to read through a plan for information literacy, but it will have a major impact on them once the program is in place. If there are new requirements to fulfill and a specific time frame for doing so, they will want to know. Keep them in mind as possible readers of the plan and create a version or a summary with their interests in mind.

IL in Action @ URI

At URI, the version of the plan we use is the only version we have at this point. It contains all the nuts and bolts, all the details. We opted to create one master document as an efficiency measure. From this document, we can tailor our document for specific uses in other departments and subject areas.

Potential Students and Their Parents

When considering academic institutions, many students and their parents look for information about the library and its programs. Your plan could have a major impact on potential students' decisions to attend your institution.

Other Offices at Your Institution

Does your institution have a development office? Its job is to show potential donors examples of the substance of your institution. Your plan for information literacy will explain a program that could be highlighted to potential donors. Perhaps a version with charts and graphs would be in order? Expected outcomes and benefits to students should also be included.

Alumni

This group frequently acts in a recruitment capacity. They may advise new students about life at your institution. Will they be interested in reading your plan? Will they be able to meaningfully translate your plan to new students? Will they recognize the benefits to students?

Future Employers

Recruiters and others looking for new employees want "information literate" graduates. Your plan should provide evidence that your institution is making an effort to provide employers with the kinds of employees they are seeking. The benefits of hiring an information literate graduate should be outlined in detail.

You want people to read your plan. Different groups have different priorities. Students want to know different things about information literacy than do administrators who may be funding the new program. We have listed some possible audiences for your document. Brainstorm possibilities for your institution and note them below.

Instructions: Brainstorm some possible audiences for your plan.

Institutional administration:

_____

_____

_____

_____

Library administration:

_____

_____

_____

_____

Faculty:

_____

_____

_____

_____

Students:

_____

_____

_____

_____

Potential students and their parents:

_____

_____

_____

_____

Offices on campus:

_____

_____

Worksheet 2-C. Ascertain the Audience for the Plan

_____

_____

Alumni:

_____

_____

_____

_____

Future employers:

_____

_____

_____

_____

Worksheet 2-C. Ascertain the Audience for the Plan
(*Continued*)

2.4.2 DETERMINE WHAT YOUR READERS WANT TO KNOW AND IN WHAT DETAIL

Now that you have identified the audiences you want to reach, it is important to supply them with the level of information they are likely to want. What will readers of your information literacy plan want to know? Will they want a general outline or will they want every detail? Will they want to know the history of traditional library instruction compared with what is needed today? Will they want to know how the plan fits into the university structure in general or will they require the specifics of course numbers, departments, and faculty?

You might want to consider creating several versions of your plan, an executive summary, a synopsis for the general public, and an in-depth explanation. Different versions for students recruiters, and employers, coupled with charts and graphs—this may not be as hard to accomplish as you imagine. Think hot links!

Listed below are several examples of what we mean by different versions and levels of interest and the most likely audience for information at various levels. It may be wise to create an electronic document that links readers to each part of the whole.

Everything from A to Z

Some groups will want and need to know all the details of the plan and how it will work; they will be most intimately involved in approving and/or implementing the program. Librarians who will be teaching library instruction sections or collaborating with other faculty to incorporate information literacy into their curriculum will want to know all the details.

Goals and Objectives

Some groups may only need to have a general sense of what you want to do and how you plan to do it. They will want to know what your plan hopes to accomplish. A curriculum or program committee might be interested in knowing about your plan at this level. Boards of higher education, school committees, and strategic planning groups may also want this kind of information.

How Information Literacy Fits into My Institution

A general summary of how the program fits in with already existing programs may be sufficient for those not directly involved. This will provide a sense of the program's place in the institution. Parents might want information about where information literacy fits into a university education. Parents of middle school students might want to know where your plan appears in middle school curriculums.

Specifics of Which Courses, Programs, and Groups Will Pilot the Information Literacy Program

People will want to know how your new plan will affect them, and when. They may want to know what to look for at a particular point in time. Some groups may want to know where to find specific courses, modules, or tutorials, and how those courses will fit into the general scheme of things. Again, providing this information will afford a sense of what others might need to do to and where new elements might be inserted. For example, if information literacy instruction is given in the fifth grade, sixth grade teachers may want to plan to build on what their incoming class already knows.

Who Will Deliver the Program

Everyone will want to know what it will mean in terms of his or her own workload. Your plan should answer this question. It should also show that you have considered the impact of this aspect of your plan. Make sure you have the full support of anyone to whom you will be giving additional work.

Departments/Colleges Affected

Every department in your institution will want to know if and how your plan might affect them. Present the information so others will see that what you are offering is an opportunity, rather than a new burden. If you expect students' term papers to improve, make sure you include that information in the document written for the people who assign the term papers.

Expected Learning Outcomes

Some groups will want to know why this plan is a good idea and what will result from it. For every new idea that comes along, people want to know what it will do for them. What can they expect to know after receiving information literacy instruction? How will it benefit them? How will they know that they know? Learning outcomes will be of interest to students, administrators, and accrediting teams.

Expected Timelines

Most likely, everyone will want to know how long a process is being undertaken in order to make adjustments in their own plans or for myriad other reasons. Students will want to know when they can start signing up for classes, employers will want to know when they can start hiring information literacy-trained employees, parents will want to know whether their child will receive information literacy instruction before graduating from high school.

Plans for Assessment/Evaluation

Many groups will want to know how you will be able to tell whether your program is getting the desired results. How will you assess competency? How will you acknowledge successful achievement?

Budget and Personnel

Administrators will want to know how much will each piece of the plan will cost and how many people will be involved. Will they be new hires or will existing personnel do the work? Will additional classrooms be required? What new equipment will be needed? Is there a plan in place for funding the initiative or do you expect the institution to find the money for you?

Students might want to know what classes they can take and what graduation requirements those classes will satisfy. Administrators will want to know how many new positions will be needed and how much each new program will cost to implement and maintain. The development office will want to know how having an information literary plan will encourage donors to give money to the institution. Think about what information your readers might want and plan to provide that information for them. We have suggested some possible levels of information below.

Instructions: Brainstorm about what every category of reader will want to know.

Everything from A to Z:

_____
_____
_____
_____

Only goals and objectives:

_____
_____
_____
_____

How information literacy fits into my institution:

_____
_____
_____
_____

Specifics of which courses, programs, and groups will pilot the information literacy program:

_____
_____
_____
_____

Who will be involved in delivering the program:

_____
_____

Worksheet 2-D. Determine What Your Readers Want to Know and in What Detail

Departments/colleges affected:

_____

_____

_____

_____

Expected learning outcomes:

_____

_____

_____

_____

Expected timelines:

_____

_____

_____

_____

Plans for assessment/evaluation:

_____

_____

_____

_____

Worksheet 2-D. Determine What Your Readers Want to Know and in What Detail (_Continued_)

2.5 ESTABLISH TIMETABLE FOR COMPLETION OF WRITTEN PLAN

You may receive a mandated timetable for completion. For example, your library director may ask you to have a completed document to him/her by the beginning of the coming fiscal year. If you are not given a set date, you will have to set your own. There are many variables to consider in setting a completion date. Try to leave enough time to allow for the unexpected, but do not allow so much time that the project never gets completed!

2.5.1 INVESTIGATE INSTITUTIONAL TIMELINES

Discover the chain of command at your institution. How do things happen? When do committees meet? What are the busiest times of the year and when are you most likely to get the attention of the people you need? Your institution probably has an organizational chart listing the chain of command. Your college and/or department may also have its own internal chain of command. You may have to follow several different routes, depending on which part of your plan you have in mind. If you know to whom to route your plan, and if you have this information when you start writing, you will be better prepared to send the appropriate parts of your plan to the appropriate people at the appropriate time. If you do not follow the chain of command, your plan will get held up, ignored, or denied because deadlines were missed.

Below are some reporting structures you might want to think about, so you can correctly time the writing, approval, and reporting of your progress along the way.

Internal Structure

In order to propose a three-credit course at URI, it had to be developed and approved in-house through our existing committee structure. You may also have to pass your work through an in-house approval hierarchy before showing it to anyone else. Work within your own committee structure and timelines.

Library Administration

All approvals from within the library should include the necessary endorsement from the library's administration. It would be good to know when your library director is available to read and discuss your document. As the work that goes beyond the library will reflect on the library itself, the director will want to read, edit, refine, and/or approve it before the document goes any further.

Institutional Committees, Faculty Senates, or School Boards

By identifying the organizational scheme, governing bodies, and supportive individuals at your institution, you will improve your odds of successfully establishing your program and your plan. The information you are seeking may not exist in writing, but rather in practice. If you do not know who is in charge, or which office handles what kind of transaction, ask until you get the answer. Leave plenty of time to find out what you need to know. You may assign someone from your writing group to concentrate on the timetable.

Institutional Administration

You want the seal of approval from the highest levels. Whether you need an official approval from your institutional administration, you will want to have their support and assistance. Make sure they know what you are up to. A good program will provide the administration with good talking points when they contact potential students, donors, partners, and local newspapers. Be very sure they know about and approve of your plan.

IL in Action @ URI

Important pieces of URI's information literacy plan had to be approved by other governing bodies at the university. For example, establishing the credit course was as big a job as developing the plan. It was sent from the library to the university curriculum committee and faculty senate within their time frame and structure for doing so. Discovering their procedure and timing for presenting our proposed course to the university for approval was critical to the success of our entire plan. If we had missed the deadlines, our plan would have been set back an entire semester. Proposing the credit course as a general education option for undergraduates meant going through the process again to explain and justify how and why it qualified for such a designation.

What is the structure of your institution? What chain of command exists? When do decisions get made? You want to be sure that the president of the university or the state board of education will be on hand when your plan is ready for approval. Listed below are some ideas about approval and due dates that we considered. You may identify other possibilities.

Instructions: Brainstorm ideas about who will need to approve your plan and when that could happen. Note your ideas below.

Internal library approval needed and when they meet:

_____

_____

_____

_____

Library administration approval needed and when they meet:

_____

_____

_____

_____

Institutional faculty committee and/or senate approval needed and when they meet:

_____

_____

_____

_____

Institutional administration approval needed and when they meet:

_____

_____

_____

_____

Board of Governors or School Board approval and when they meet:

_____

_____

_____

_____

Worksheet 2-E. Establish Who Needs to Approve the Plan and by What Due Date

2.5.2 ESTABLISH A TIMETABLE FOR COMPLETION OF THE WRITTEN PLAN

Consider the members of your writing group, the number of times you can realistically meet, your approval processes, and so on. Then gauge how much writing you think you will be able to do in a set period of time, for example, in six months. Do not try to do more than you have time for. Be realistic about how long it is going to take. If your writing group can only meet once a month, it may take some time to put a plan together. You might want to think about to how you can move the process along. Can you meet electronically? Can you exchange drafts via e-mail? Can you get feedback from other groups without actually meeting face to face? Try to plan for the most efficient and effective means of getting the plan written. If you think about it beforehand, you may come up with some creative ideas to solve the meeting problem.

Listed below are some goals you might consider trying to reach during the first six months of writing the plan.

Create a Draft Plan for Information Literacy

If you have done all the planning suggested up to this point, you should have some idea of whom you will be working with, what kind of meetings you will have, who will be on your writing team, how often you will be able to meet, what approval deadlines you have, and what printing deadlines (for listing courses in the college catalog, getting information into new student packets, monthly newsletters, for example) you will have to meet. With this information, you should be able to estimate how long you will need to create a draft plan. The more complex your institution, the more time consuming the process may be.

Supply a Draft Plan to Appropriate Library Committees and Administrators

If you can write a draft plan in six months, can you also get it to one or more groups for comment and/or approval? Go back to your academic calendar and your organizational chart. Look at the due dates for new program submissions, find out who has to approve your plan before it can be approved by the new program committee, and determine whether you can meet the deadline.

Get the Document to Committees at Appropriate Time

Again, if you pay careful attention to the deadlines of other groups and committees your process will move along more quickly. Will you be able to

---

IL in Action @ URI

At URI, we submitted our first draft plan to the Public Services Committee in 2000. We submitted our final draft to the library faculty in 2002. With presentations to various groups, revisions, additions, and changes, it took eighteen months to create a plan that was acceptable to everyone. We felt it was well worth the time it took. In the end, we had a document everyone could support and use.

get your draft plan to all the necessary committees in six months? Nobody wants to be on a task force with a never-ending task. Setting a reasonable estimate of how long it will take to get a document through the committee stage will mentally prepare writing team members for the length of time they will be working on this project.

Get Feedback and Make Revisions

Do you think you can create the draft plan, get it out to other groups for input and make revisions so that your revised draft plan can make the rounds again in the time allowed? The complexity of your plan will probably determine this as well.

Planning to write is a major part of the planning process. Once you have all your questions answered about who will do the writing, when they will do it, where the writing will take place, what will be written, and in what order, to whom the drafts will go for approval, the writing group(s) will be free to concentrate on writing the plan.

3

WRITE THE PLAN

INTRODUCTION

Writing the plan is a big job. Like any other major task, it may seem daunting. If you have been directed to write a plan and the project has a clear, expected implementation date, you will undoubtedly feel empowered during the writing process. Some plan writers, however, may be required to create a plan without the absolute knowledge that approval is imminent or attainable. If that is the case, you may have to provide your own deadlines and goals. If your plan is being written in order to prepare a convincing proposal to other constituencies so that you can establish an information literacy program, having a thoughtful and completed plan will go a long way toward supporting your goal. Remember that the plan will be extremely helpful in explaining what you want to accomplish and why. The plan will also inform your audience about how, when, and where you want to accomplish the delivery of your IL program.

Putting your plan in writing is not that much different from doing any other big job. We suggest that you write an outline of what you intend to include in the plan and then write one section at a time. Do not be overwhelmed by the thought of writing the entire plan. Take small steps and work to complete parts of the plan. Perhaps in your planning to write you have already taken care of this step by assigning different parts of the writing to different members of the writing committee. Keep track of what you have accomplished and what still needs to be done. You can look at the big picture when you have made some progress in writing some parts of the plan.

3.1 LEARN THE KEY POINTS OF THE PLAN

What should and could go into the plan? Think about whom you want to reach and what you need to include so that the plan can be understood by all members of your audience. Think about the questions that others might ask you in person if you tell them you are writing a comprehensive plan for information literacy. For example, if I told a friend I was going to write a report on stochastic calculus, the first question my friend might ask is, "What's that?" One part of my report would be a definition of the topic. After defining the topic, my friend might ask, "Why would anybody want to learn about stochastic calculus?" So another part of my report would explain why the topic is important or meaningful. If you follow this train of thought you will come up with the major questions your plan needs to answer.

A basic plan should include the following sections:

1. An introduction that includes a definition of IL and other terms, scope of the program (how broad), definitions of other nonstandard terms and acronyms, why they are important, and how much information is available (information explosion/anxiety) (See Part II, Section 5.1 for an explanation of these terms)

2. A history of trends in library instruction and instructional programs at your institution

3. The goals and objectives of your program

4. The body of your plan

5. Oversight

6. Methods of assessment

7. A timeline for implementation of the plan

8. Marketing plan

In Step 3, we will explore each of the above-mentioned items.

3.1.1 THE INTRODUCTION: WHAT IS IN A NAME?

In your planning group(s), one of your first jobs will be to agree on the name for the plan you want to use and know why it is an appropriate term for your institution. Many libraries use the term information literacy. There are other terms, however, that are used, for example, information competence and information fluency. These three terms are used interchangeably and although the definition of each varies, there is no real difference among them. Use whichever term is locally recognized by a regional accrediting agency or other institutions in your area, and be consistent in using the term you have selected throughout your document.

The differences among the terms in use seem to be more attributable to the mission and goals of each organization, as well as to the time (when institutions chose a term) and geographic location (where each term was most frequently in use) of the discussion than disagreement about the meaning of the basic terms.

Many regional accrediting bodies now require institutions to show evidence of instruction and assessment of information literacy in the curriculum. Therefore, review the requirements of your regional accrediting body and find out what term they use for information literacy. Find out what is going on locally and regionally. You may find that the best term to use is not the first one that comes to mind. You will want to use the term most generally known and most locally accepted. Understanding is the goal— you want your readers to understand what you are talking about. If you use the term or terms most easily recognized by your reading audiences, you will keep their interest and avoid confusion. Some of the requirements for accrediting agencies are listed below.

Accrediting Agencies

Middle States Association of Colleges and Schools
http://www.msache.org/
See Publications, Eligibility Requirements for Standards for Accreditation, 2002
See Standard 11, Educational Offerings

NEASC—New England Association of Colleges and Schools
www.neasc.org/cihe/stancihe.htm
www.neasc.org/cihe/revisions/draft_standards_for_accreditation.pdf
See draft Standard 7.4
See draft Standard 4.6

Northwest Association of Colleges and Schools
http://www.nwccu.org/
See Accreditation Standards, Standard 2.A.8

Southern Association of Schools and Colleges
www.sacscoc.org/pdf/principles%20of%20accreditation1.pdf
See Section 3.8.2

For a list of various accrediting agencies you may wish to consult the following Web sites:

http://airweb.org/links/accred.cfm
www.degree.net/guides/gaap_listings.html

Select a Term for Information Literacy

Information literacy is a pedagogical framework that addresses efficient and effective information research. People must be accomplished at finding/gathering, evaluating/analyzing, and applying/using information appropriately.

ALA (1989), Shapiro and Hughes (1996), and the ACRL (1993) have all created information literacy definitions that focus primarily on critical thinking concepts that are supported by the need for students to attain sufficient technology skills for the information age.

As the American Library Association Presidential Committee on Information Literacy (January 10, 1989, Washington, DC) states, "Ultimately, information literate people are those who have learned how to learn. They know how to learn because they know: how knowledge is organized, how to find information, and how to use information in such a way that others can learn from them. They are people prepared for lifelong learning, because they can always find the information needed for any task or decision at hand."

Jeremy J. Shapiro and Shelley K. Hughes (1996) provide a more detailed definition of information literacy in their article "Information Literacy as a Liberal Art." Briefly put, Shapiro and Hughes make the following major points in their definition:

- In its narrowest sense information literacy includes the practical skills involved in effective use of information technology and information resources, either print or electronic.
- Information literacy is a new liberal art that extends beyond technical skills and is conceived as the critical reflection on the nature of information itself, its technical infrastructure, and its social, cultural, and even philosophical context and impact.
- The information literacy curriculum includes:
    - Tool literacy—The ability to use print and electronic resources including software.
    - Resource literacy—The ability to understand the form, format, location, and access methods of information resources.
    - Social-structural literacy—Knowledge of how information is socially situated and produced. It includes understanding the scholarly publishing process.
    - Research literacy—The ability to understand and use information technology tools to carry out research including discipline-related software.

- Publishing literacy—The ability to produce a text or multimedia report of the results of research.

Information Fluency

Information fluency is considered to be the seamless understanding or fluency acquired by the researcher of both information resources and information technology. This concept is a bow to the technology world—to be adept at research one must be a knowledgeable and savvy computer user. Daniel Callison (2003, 38–39) writes, "A reasonable definition at this time: information fluency is the ability to analyze information needs and to move confidently among media, information, and computer literacy skills resulting in the effective application of a strategy or strategies that will best meet those needs."

Information Competence

California State University developed the following definition of information competence in 1997. They chose to define the term by listing the competencies that describe it:

A Set of Core Competencies

In order to be able to find, evaluate, use, communicate, and appreciate information in all its various formats, students must be able to demonstrate the following skills:

1. Define the research topic.
2. Determine the information requirements for the research question, problem, or issue.
3. Locate and retrieve relevant information.
4. Organize and synthesize information.
5. Communicate using a variety of information technologies.
6. Understand ethical, legal, and socio-political issues surrounding information and information technology.
7. Use, evaluate, and treat critically information received from the mass media.

Definition of Information Literacy

Your introduction should include the definition of information literacy. Make sure your definition clearly states what information literacy means (or will mean) at your institution. The definition that best suits your institution will be tailored to what you do and how you do it. A boilerplate definition may not address the specific needs of your institution.

Do not assume that everyone at your institution knows what information literacy is or knows what you mean when you use the term. When you are immersed in a topic it is easy to forget that others may not know the first thing about it. Just as a master plumber might have to define a pipe wrench in order to talk to you about repairing your kitchen sink, you must begin by defining your terms to your audience of readers so they will understand the steps that follow.

As a starting point, you may wish to consult one or more of the many definitions of information literacy that are available. There are national, international, and industry definitions that are applicable to library, K-12, higher education, business, and other settings. The definition or definitions that you choose to work with should be aligned with your program and the goals of your institution.

Following is a list of sources for both information literacy definitions and models of information literacy from a variety of national and international organizations. Review these for possible use, keeping in mind your institution's overall mission and goals and any colleges, grade levels, or programs on which you are planning to focus. Consider writing your local definition by combining ideas from an institution type (e.g., higher education) and focusing the plan by introducing ideas using discipline or industry standards (e.g., science and technology) to create an information literacy plan that meets your overall situation.

National and International Definitions

ALA—American Library Association.
Presidential Committee on Information Literacy. Final Report. January 1989.
www.ala.org/ala/acrl/acrlpubs/whitepapers/presidential.htm
"Ultimately, information literate people are those who have learned how to learn. They know how to learn because they know how knowledge is organized, how to find information, and how to use information in such a way that others can learn from them. They are people prepared for lifelong learning, because they can always find the information needed for any task or decision at hand."

Definitions, Standards and Competencies from NFIL
www.infolit.org/definitions/index.html

NFIL Definitions, Standards, and Competencies Related to Information Literacy refers to a constellation of skills revolving around information research and use. According to the Final Report of the American Library Association Presidential Committee on Information Literacy (1989), the information literate person is "able to recognize when information is needed and have the ability to locate, evaluate, and use it effectively."

NFIL—National Forum for Information Literacy
www.infolit.org
"Information Literacy is defined as the ability to know when there is a need for information, to be able to identify, locate, evaluate, and effectively use that information for the issue or problem at hand."

Definitions Related to Information Literacy

> Business Literacy: The ability to use financial and business information to understand and make decisions that help an organization achieve success.
>
> Computer Literacy: The ability to use a computer and its software to accomplish practical tasks.
>
> Health Literacy: The degree to which individuals have the capacity to obtain, process, and understand basic health information and services needed to make appropriate health decisions.
>
> Information Literacy: The ability to know when there is a need for information, to be able to identify, locate, evaluate, and effectively use that information for the issue or problem at hand.
>
> Media Literacy: The ability to decode, analyze, evaluate, and produce communication in a variety of forms.
>
> Technology Literacy: The ability to use media such as the Internet to effectively access and communicate information.
>
> Visual Literacy: The ability, through knowledge of the basic visual elements, to understand the meaning and components of the image.

For additional terms and definitions, visit "Definitions of Information Literacy and Related Terms" from the University of South Florida (August 2003), www.infolit.org/definitions/.

Information Literacy Standards and Competencies

For Students:
For K-12:

The Nine Information Literacy Standards for Student Learning. From the American Association of School Librarians and Association for Educational Communications Technology.
www.ala.org/ala/aasl/aaslproftools/informationpower/informationliteracy
.htm

For Higher Education:

Information Literacy Competency Standards for Higher Education. From the Association of College and Research Libraries.
www.ala.org/ala/acrl/acrlstandards/informationliteracycompetency.htm

Related Information Literacy Web Sites

Australia and New Zealand
Australian and New Zealand Information Literacy Framework and Principles standards and practice, 2nd edition, edited by Alan Bundy.
www.anziil.org/resources/Info%201it%202nd%20edition.pdf

The Big Blue—funded by the Joint Information Systems Committee and managed jointly by Manchester Metropolitan University Library and Leeds University Library. Big Blue Final Report, July 2002 (full).
www.library.mmu.ac.uk/bigblue/finalreportful.html

Compiled by Dane Ward, Illinois State University Library. National Forum on Information Literacy
www.infolit.org/related_sites/
This site is a compilation that includes general information Web sites, college and university Web sites, a list from ACRL's Institute of Information Literacy of information literacy competencies, international programs and projects, models of instruction, professional organizations, tutorials, related concepts, and health literacy Web sites.

IFLA—International Federation of Library Associations and Institutions
Information Literacy Section
www.ifla.org/VII/s42/index.htm
NOTE: As of this writing, the IFLA Information Literacy project is working to draft international guidelines on information literacy.

For Higher Education:

ACRL—Association of College and Research Libraries
Information Literacy Overview
www.ala.org/ala/acrl/acrlissues/acrlinfolit/infolitoverview/introtoinfolit
/introinfolit.htm

ACRL Information Literacy Competency Standards for Higher Education
www.ala.org/ala/acrl/acrlstandards/informationliteracycompetency.htm

SCONUL—Society of College, National and University Libraries
Standing Conference of National and University Libraries
The Seven Pillars of Information Literacy
www.sconul.ac.uk/activities/inf_lit/seven_pillars.html

For K-12 Schools:

AASL—Association of School Librarians
Information Literacy Standards for Student Learning
www.ala.org/aaslTemplate.cfm?Section=informationpower&Template=
/ContentManagement/ContentDisplay.cfm&ContentID=19937

The Big6—Michael Eisenberg
www.big6.com/

Information Power
www.ala.org/aala/aasl/proftools/informationpower/informationpower
.htm

Examples of Information Literacy in the Disciplines

Science and Technology:

ACRL—Science and Technology Section
Task Force on Information Literacy for Science and Technology
Proposed Information Literacy Standards
http://sciencelibrarian.tripod.com/ILTaskForce/ILIndex.htm

Social Science:

APA
"What Psych Majors Need to Know" by Bridget Murray
Monitor on Psychology 33(7), July/August 2002, p. 80.
www.apa.org/monitor/julaug02/psychmajors.html
See standard no. 6

Humanities:

Research Competency Guidelines for Literatures in English
ACRL, Literatures in English Section, October 2004.
www.ala.org/ala/acrl/acrlstandards/researchcompentenciesLES.htm

Examples of Information Literacy in Business and Industry

Information Industry Literacy within the New Millennium: A Case Study
of a Developing Country—Egypt.—Shawky Salem, July 2002.
White paper prepared for UNESCO, the U.S. National
Commission on Libraries and Information Science, and the
National Forum on Information Literacy for use at the
Information Literacy Meeting of Experts. Prague, The Czech
Republic. Available at:
www.nclis.gov/libinter/infolitconf&meet/papers/salem-
fullpaper.pdf

> We are no longer teaching about technology, but
> about information literacy . . . Students need the think-
> ing, reasoning, and civic abilities that enable them to
> succeed in a contemporary democratic economy,
> workforce and society.—Terry Crane, Vice President
> for Educational Products, AOL, September 2000 is-
> sue of *Converge*.

> [t]he bottom line is that to be successful, you need to
> acquire a high level of information literacy. What we
> need in the knowledge industries are people who
> know how to absorb and analyze and integrate and
> create and effectively convey information—and who
> know how to use information to bring value to every-
> thing they undertake.—Anthony Comper, President
> of the Bank of Montreal, 1999 commencement ad-
> dress at University of Toronto.

To find examples of definitions for information literacy you may want to
refer to some Web sites from the library profession.

ACRL Information Literacy—Best Practices Web Site (www.ala
.org/ala/acrl/acrlstandards/characteristics.htm) and ACRL (www.ala.org/
ala/acrl/acrlstandards/informationliteracycompetency.htm#ildef) have information literacy definitions that focus primarily on critical thinking concepts that are supported by the need for students to attain sufficient
understanding of the information research process in combination with
competent information technology skills with which to do research in the
information age.

Consider how broad your program is going to be. Will you include fluency with technology per se as part of your information literacy plan /definition? Will you include instruction in how to use the computer to do various tasks along with IL instruction? Does that task already belong to another group or could your plan be used to provide instruction that does not now exist? Could you work cooperatively with another group to make sure that both information technology and information literacy are acquired in a logical and progressive manner?

Your accrediting organization might also specify what needs to be included. If your plan is truly institution-wide, you might be able to divide responsibilities for different aspects of information literacy to different parts of your organization. For example, the library might be responsible for information literacy; the institutional technology department might be responsible for computer programs and applications and how to use them, while the writing faculty might cover the organization and presentation of ideas. At an institution with more integrated technology, you may have to include more in the plan because you are responsible for tasks beyond knowledge content. Collaborate with departments as necessary and useful in your situation.

School libraries might choose to address only some of the standards for information literacy, knowing that more advanced concepts will be covered when students reach higher levels of education and have a need for more advanced research skills.

> ## IL in Action @ URI
>
> In our experience, because we are our own college at URI, we chose only to address the knowledge content part of information literacy. We chose not to address technology skills because another department on campus was already doing the computer skills component. The new standards for accreditation for our regional accrediting agency, NEASC, may require that we change or broaden our plan to include information technology under our plan's umbrella.

Examples of Information Literacy for Professionals

Different professions have definitions or competency requirements for information literacy skills. For example, engineering, nursing, and architecture have specific and directed needs concerning information literacy. The licensing agencies governing these professions may have their own standards for information literacy. If you are writing a plan for a library supporting a professional program you will want to look at the profession in question and find out what they require in terms of information literacy.

Task Force on Undergraduate Psychology Major Competencies. 2002. *Undergraduate Psychology Major Learning Goals and Outcomes: A Report.* Washington, DC: American Psychological Association. Available: www.apa.org/ed/pcue/taskforcereport2.pdf (accessed: July 18, 2005).

This document represents the work of the Task Force on Undergraduate Psychology Major Competencies appointed by the American Psychological Association's Board of Educational Affairs. The document outlines ten goals and suggested learning outcomes that represent reasonable departmental expectations for the undergraduate psychology major across educational contexts.

The goals are divided into two major categories: (1) Knowledge, skills, and values consistent with the science and application of psychology and (2) Knowledge, skills, and values consistent with liberal arts education that are further developed in psychology. See section 6.1 of the document for more information. The document concludes with a preliminary discussion of assessment principles and a proposal for developing appropriate assessment strategies based on the Undergraduate Psychology Learning Goals and Outcomes. This next step will be critical in promoting high quality learning experiences in the undergraduate psychology major.

Similarly, dentists need to "evaluate scientific literature and other sources of information to make decisions about dental treatment" (*Journal of Dental Education* 67, no. 7, 2). Nurses should have critical thinking skills that will enable them to "integrate pertinent data from multiple sources" (www.nursingworld.org/mods/archive/mod110/copa3.htm.)

Once you have developed your definition of information literacy, share it with the other stakeholders at your institution. Make sure that you have a broad-based agreement within your library and/or your institution about the definition before you include it in the plan.

Definitions of Other Nonstandard Terms and Acronyms

You will be sharing your plan with others beyond your immediate working group. It is important to use language that a general reader can understand. It is difficult for anyone to read a document that is filled with jargon and acronyms. You do not want your reader to lose interest because the inclusion of acronyms makes the reading process too slow or too confusing.

Be sure to spell out all acronyms, at least the first time they are used. If you find it necessary to use a large number of acronyms it may be necessary to include the complete name every time. Define any terms that are not part of the average nonlibrarian's vocabulary. This will require that you think about the kinds of words the average person knows and what those words mean in a nonlibrary context. Are there words with multiple meanings that could confuse rather than enlighten the reader? Consider including a glossary at the end of your plan that includes common terms and acronyms to which nonpractitioners can refer.

Why Is Information Literacy Important to the Future of All Students?

Once they understand the definition, your readers should ask why information literacy is important. Create a document that justifies the need for your program. Spell out what this program is designed to do and how it meets the identified needs.

The following is an example of how you could explain to nonpractitioners just why information literacy is so important.

> The time we live in is known as the information age. This is so because of the remarkable amount of information that has become easily available to the average person. Anyone who has access to the Internet can get information from numerous sources on just about any topic. There are many sources and many formats for information above and beyond the tools that have been available for the past 500 years or so. We are in fact bombarded with information from television, radio, movies, the Internet, billboards, magazines, newspapers, bulletin boards, chat rooms, blogs, and government reports.

As the amount of information grows and the number of sources supplying that information expands, information overload results. People become confused and overwhelmed by the sheer amount of information. A quick Internet search on a general subject will demonstrate this fact admirably. How can anyone find and select the specific piece of information wanted when faced with millions of Web sites, newspaper articles, government documents, and personal Web pages on the topic?

Having too much information is almost as bad as having no information at all. For those seeking answers to questions that may affect the way they live their lives or how they make important decisions on unknown topics, having too much information results in information anxiety. People get stuck and fearful. How can they find an answer they can trust? How can they select the right information from among the large number of choices they have?

Below we have listed items included in the introduction to our plan. You may want to include other ideas or additional concepts. Customize your introduction to fit your institution.

Instructions: Brainstorm ideas and concepts you want to include in your introduction.

Definition of information literacy:

_____

_____

_____

_____

Definitions of other nonstandard terms and acronyms:

_____

_____

_____

_____

Why information literacy is important to the future of all students:

_____

_____

_____

_____

Worksheet 3-A. Customize the Introduction

3.1.2 HISTORY OF TRENDS AT YOUR INSTITUTION

Remember that your plan may be read by people who know very little about how your work is done. Put what you do in perspective so that readers get the big picture. Make sure that your readers understand the major changes that have taken place in the world during the last ten to fifteen years and how those changes affect doing library business in an academic setting.

The following is an example of how you could tell people what changes have taken place in libraries and how that affects doing library business.

In the not-too-distant past, there were relatively few options for obtaining information. One could use books, journals, government reports, and personal contacts to research a given topic and acquire information. Today, we are faced with a vast number of choices in terms of where and how we get the information we use. The online environment has provided us with all kinds of information that was previously unavailable. It has also provided us with all kinds of biased and unreliable information from named and unnamed sources all over the world.

People seeking information want and need to be more independent. The availability of information online means that people search for and find information when they are not in the library building. This means that there are fewer librarian-mediated searches. People doing research outside the library do not have the benefit of the search skills and familiarity with keywords, subject headings, and search engines that a librarian might be able to provide to the person working on site. Often, searchers lack the knowledge and/or skills necessary to create and complete a good search in the online environment. For this reason, everyone searching for information needs some instruction in how to use the available online tools. As the tools continue to change, everyone will need to know how to keep their skills and knowledge current.

The World Wide Web is an unmediated source of information. Information found on the Web can and does come from anywhere and anyone. An individual does not have to be an expert on a topic to post information on that topic to a Web site. Biased points of view are expressed on Web sites and at times intentionally misleading and incorrect information is posted. People also use the Web to play jokes on others. On the otherhand, scholars and scientists can post their research findings to Web sites. Health organizations and government agencies create Web sites for the improvement of the lives of the people they serve. People can find long lost relatives and stay in touch with friends around the world too. The point is that there is no Internet police department. People can create Web sites and put any kind of information they want on those sites. While this freedom of speech is wonderful in its own way, it puts the onus of evaluation of information on the user. Just as in the past people were warned not to believe everything they read in the newspaper, today people must be aware that evaluation of the merits, accuracy, reliability, authority, and currency of information on the Web is essential. So much information is available, but each and every Web page must be examined to determine its usefulness in providing needed information.

How Libraries Have Changed

To put your plan into perspective, you may want to explain how libraries and library users have changed as technology has changed. For example, people used to stand at the reference desk and ask questions. Now they call, e-mail, fax, chat, *and* stand at the desk. Information seekers used to use a

IL in Action

In an institution that already has a strong bibliographic instruction program, it may be necessary to adapt the information covered during these sessions. In order to address the recent changes and resulting needs of library users, it may be necessary to change what information is delivered during a typical BI session. The librarian could systematize the presentation (create a set script, make a Power Point slide show, or videotape the content of the BI sessions to be delivered, for example) while incorporating information literacy concepts rather than how-to instruction. With these tools, instruction could reach more students (perhaps by allowing TA's or library staff to conduct BI sessions).

IL in Action

Carol Ansel, at Pine Point School in Stonington, Connecticut, has created several hands-on exercises at grade-appropriate levels to demonstrate the need for evaluation of information coupled with a checklist of things to look for. The time spent providing this information may replace a lesson given in the past, such as using a paper index to find a citation to a journal article.

fairly limited set of resources—books and journals in paper format. They needed to be where the resources resided. Today, there are many choices of format, many options for access and delivery, and sometimes no need to be on site to use the materials. The Web, for example, is a source of information that many students use, but the content of many resources is beyond the control of the library and/or academic community. The quality of information is also very uneven and not always suitable for academic purposes. Students must be taught how to evaluate what they find so they can identify appropriate sources of information.

How Your Library Has Changed

The increase in demand for teaching in the library and/or from the library has increased exponentially in many libraries. Describing this change will underscore the need for your program. Do not be afraid to restate the obvious in your plan! What is clear to you may be news to your readers.

Inform readers of the changing nature of library use, user education, and reference. Illustrate your points with statistics and anecdotes to drive your subject home. Describe what you do, how it has been accomplished in the past, and why you need to shift your practice to a program that better meets the needs of today's users. It is important to set the stage so readers will understand the need for the program.

For example, a student at the reference desk may require instruction in using a database that is time consuming and labor intensive. Also, because that database provides so much data with relatively little effort, the student needs to be able to filter through the results to find what is most relevant. The focus of the information search of today has changed. As a result, assistance from the reference librarian must also be different. There is a growing trend that shows that instruction happens more often than ever before as part of every reference transaction.

What You Already Do

Most institutions provide basic instruction in how to use the library. Some institutions have extensive instructional programs in place in which they teach students in the library or in their classrooms.

Whether it is traditional bibliographic instruction or one-on-one assistance at the reference desk, in this section of your plan make sure to acknowledge and catalog everything you already do that supports the goals of information literacy. This will show your readers that information literacy is not entirely new to the library. Some parts of your program already exist. You have been offering instruction for a long time and addressing the needs of your library users in a specific learning environment. You may already be addressing some or all of the information literacy competencies as part of your existing instructional program. Be sure to explain what you already do. Later in the document you will explain how changing technologies and changing research strategies create new and unmet needs that to be addressed.

Esther Grassian, Information Literacy Outreach Coordinator at UCLA, recently outlined the similarities between bibliographic instruction and information literacy. She offers a brief history of bibliographic instruction, along with the changes that changed the delivery of that type of instruction. She includes an excellent summary on the rationale for moving library instruction programs from a bibliographic instruction approach to a more fully developed information literacy program. Consider Grassian's comments in the October 2004 edition of *American Libraries* (vol. 35, no. 9: 51–53):

> I see information literacy not as a wholly new and different approach, but as an umbrella that encompasses and expands on the BI efforts we've all been engaged in for many years. (p. 51)

In her conclusion she says,

> However, as we reach out, we need to respect and make good use of our rich BI experience by offering blended BI/IL instruction, with greater attention to balancing concepts and mechanics as well as instructional formats. (p. 53)

Grassian's comments emphasize the importance of explaining what parts of your instruction program already exist. This will allow your reading audience to understand the nature and scope of the changes you are proposing.

What Tools Have You Adapted in the Face of Technological or Other Changes?

Be sure to state how your current activities have evolved in response to the changing needs of library users. Of the activities you already do or have mentioned, which have you adapted to the new information environment? For example, some institutions have converted their information guides to electronic format and made them available on the Web. Others have created online tutorials.

You may want to explain that without an information literacy plan, efforts to this point have been piecemeal. In order to streamline and address all unmet needs you want to bring all instruction in information literacy under the umbrella of a comprehensive plan.

Explain what you have been doing to meet the changing demands of library instruction. Online tutorials, user guides, more BI sessions, more face-to-face interaction, e-mail or virtual reference are all things that might be described here. Tell your readers how you are responding to the changing technology and information environment.

What Needs Are Still Unmet at Your Institution?

Comparing your needs assessment with your current services is a good way to determine what unmet needs still exist. If you find that you need a comprehensive plan for information literacy, then there are unmet needs at your institution. You may find that students need critical thinking and evaluation skills. You may find that the emphasis needs to shift from knowing what buttons to push to knowing what database to select. Later in your plan, you should spell out how you will provide those skills in your information literacy program.

The Information Literacy Best Practices Project is a Web site that provides a list of ten outstanding characteristics found in information literacy programs nationwide. Check this list to help you think about unmet needs at your institution. See www.accd.edu/pac/lrc/evaluatn/infolitbest.htm.

Think about what you know about how libraries have changed during the past decade. Be aware that not everyone knows what you know. In order for "outsiders" to understand the need for your plan, what do you need to tell them? We have listed a few ideas below.

Instructions: Brainstorm about the changes that have taken place in the world and at your institution and how that affects what you do.

How has the world changed during the last decade?

_____

_____

_____

_____

How have libraries changed?

_____

_____

_____

_____

How has your library changed?

_____

_____

_____

_____

How is your library adapting existing services to the changes?

_____

_____

_____

_____

What do you do *now* that supports information literacy goals?

_____

_____

_____

_____

Worksheet 3-B. Review the History of Change in Libraries and IL

What are the still unmet needs at your institution?

_____

_____

_____

_____

Worksheet 3-B. Review the History of Change in Libraries and IL (_Continued_)

IL in Action

An engineering or technical college would look for the incorporation of scientific competencies in their plan for information literacy. Find out if there are any national standards for engineers to determine the professional requirements or recommendations for engineering graduates or practitioners. Base your list of goals and objectives on expected outcomes. A goal for engineering or technical colleges would then be to prepare their students to meet the standards established by their future profession and the accrediting body.

IL in Action @ URI

At URI, one of our specific objectives was to develop a credit course. The goal then, was to immerse students in a semester-long credit course for maximum learning.

3.1.3 GOALS AND OBJECTIVES OF YOUR PROGRAM

In this section of your plan, you will want to clearly state the goals and objectives of your information literacy program.

Your goals should encompass "the big picture." Take the future into account and everything that you would like to accomplish. In your goals, use your imagination, think broadly, and think long term. Do not let your previous practices, level of resources, or institutional barriers limit you.

In formulating your goals, refer to the information literacy standards that you have reviewed and keep your institution's mission and definition of information literacy at the forefront. While you want your goals to encompass your vision for the future, be certain that all of your goals are relevant to your situation and the mission of your institution. It may not be necessary or appropriate to include all the goals that address every possible variation of information competencies suggested at the national level. Consider which competencies you are best positioned to achieve.

Your objectives should weave together what is practical within the broad scope of your goals. They should be concrete action items that you can accomplish to help you attain each of your goals. Keep in mind that you can list multiple objectives for each goal and that objectives can be achieved incrementally. Include things that you can accomplish right away as well as those that might only be "dreams" at this point. Keep your institutional culture in mind and what you think will be acceptable to others. Do not stray too far from what your administration will accept, at least at the beginning.

3.1.4 THE BODY OF YOUR PLAN

The main part of the plan is where you lay out detailed ideas in a format that is clear, visually pleasing, and easy to follow. It will include:

(1) all levels of learners you want to reach,

(2) information you want to convey to each group,

(3) different methods and technologies you will use to accomplish your goals,

(4) personnel, space, and equipment to be used,

(5) the means by which you will assess your success,

(6) the marketing plan, and

(7) the oversight/review mechanisms for the program.

Organization of this part of the plan is discussed in detail in Step 3, section 3.2.

3.1.5 OVERSIGHT

You will want to write in detail about what lines of reporting people delivering the plan will follow. It should be made clear who is in charge of making decisions and seeing that the objectives of the plan are being met. Oversight is discussed at length in Step 4, section 4.1.

3.1.6 ASSESSMENT

Make specific plans for measuring the success of both the entire and individual parts of your plan. If you have the assessment plan ready as you implement each part of your plan, you will provide yourself with a great benefit. As parts of the plan are implemented, people become very busy delivering them, and frequently do not have time to think about designing, administering, and analyzing an assessment tool. Assessment is discussed in Step 4, section 4.2.

3.1.7 TIMELINE FOR IMPLEMENTATION

A written timeline will only be an estimate. Many variables can change the order and magnitude of the implementation of your plan. So make a timeline to keep you on track, but do not set the dates and deadlines in stone. Allow yourself enough flexibility to change your time frame if and when you need to. The timetable for implementation is discussed in Step 3, section 3.3.

3.1.8 MARKETING

Write the plan for marketing your program, based on the parts you want to implement first. Educate your audience about information literacy and how it can help meet the mission and goals of your institution. Getting the word out and convincing people of its importance are big steps in the success of your plan. Marketing is discussed in Step 4, section 4.3.

3.2 ORGANIZE THE PLAN

The body of the plan will serve as a user manual for implementing your information literacy program. You will refer to it again and again and so will everyone with a vested interest in your program. It is important to design it so it is easy to use and visually appealing.

Create a framework for the body of your plan that is modular and easy to understand. There are a number of potential ways you can organize the content of this section. You may wish to structure this part of your plan by student population, discipline, type of instruction, location of instruction, or in combination. Below, we will examine some of these possibilities.

It will be useful to think about segments of your total population with similar needs. Create a program that will meet the needs of each group if your plan calls for you to reach them all. Below are some examples of how you might organize your plan.

3.2.1 STRUCTURE YOUR PLAN BY STUDENT POPULATION (CLASS LEVEL)

Structuring your plan by student population will often mean creating a tiered program based on student level, for example, by grade in K-12, and by year in a college or university setting. If you choose this approach, first consider your student population and their levels of need. Decide at which point in their academic program would be the best time to introduce information literacy concepts. Consider how your institution structures the student learning experience. Perhaps there is a core curriculum around which you could build the information literacy program. The following is an example from the University of Rhode Island.

Information Literacy for Freshmen at the University of Rhode Island

Since 1995, we have been delivering fundamental information concepts to freshmen at the University of Rhode Island through a required course that introduced all freshmen to the university. For years, we had also been reaching freshmen through an introductory writing course that many freshmen took. We saw these courses as opportunities around which to structure our freshmen information literacy activities. We looked at what we already did in these two classes and then systematically incorporated

---

IL in Action @ URI

Suggested Implementation at URI

Freshman Year

By the end of their freshman year, all students should have mastered the introductory concepts. Many will also have been familiarized with some of the advanced concepts and will have worked with subject-specific concepts and resources and universal concepts.

URI 101/WRT 101 Modules

URI 101 and WRT (Introduction to writing) 104-105-106 modules will introduce students to the library and information-seeking skills as the first step to information literacy.
   In URI 101, students will:

- Become familiar with library building locations and service points
- Use the HELIN library catalog to locate books and journals
- Understand the concept of subject headings
- Understand Library of Congress call number sequence
- Understand the difference between a catalog and an index

   The URI 101 module will consist of in-library instruction, a librarian-graded, in-class assignment included in the overall course grade, a brief tour of the library building, and a follow-up assignment facilitated by the course instructor.
   In WRT 104-105-106, students will:

- Understand what a periodical is and learn the difference between a newspaper, popular magazine, trade publication, and scholarly journal
- Understand what a periodical index is
- Understand subject descriptors and other access points
- Use the Library's core, interdisciplinary periodical database to find journal articles

   The WRT 104-105-106 module will consist of in-library instruction, a librarian-graded, in-class assignment included in the overall course grade, and a follow-up assignment facilitated by the course instructor.
   Many of the materials for the URI 101 and WRT 104-105-106 modules will be available on the Web, and at some point an interactive Web tutorial may be developed.

---

information literacy concepts into our instruction, making both classes a central part of our comprehensive information literacy plan for first-year students.

Information Literacy for Sophomores at the University of Rhode Island

Possibilities for reaching all students at the sophomore level are not as well-defined at our institution. There are no set courses that all sophomores

---

IL in Action @ URI

Sophomore Year

By the end of their sophomore year, most students will have completed their general education requirements. During their sophomore year, they will have further opportunities to master introductory and advanced information literacy concepts and will have worked with subject-specific concepts and resources and universal concepts.

To deliver these information literacy concepts during the sophomore year, library faculty will need to work closely with the General Education Program as well as with individual departments and programs to incorporate information literacy modules into the classroom. Library faculty can also play a role in consulting with other teaching faculty on the design of research-based assignments and exercises.

---

are required to take. Some students will take introductory writing. All sophomores are working to fulfill their General Education requirements.

We decided to target General Education courses as the medium through which we could reach the majority of the sophomore class. Through collaboration with the instructors of subject-specific classes that satisfy General Education requirements, we offer advanced, "one-shot" library instruction sections covering the tools and techniques that target the content and assignment goals of the class. For example, history classes will learn about the reference tools available to history researchers.

We also created our own three-credit course that satisfies a General Education requirement in English Communication. This allows us to offer intensive instruction in information literacy in a formal classroom setting.

Although the course is not limited to sophomores, we did target sophomore year in our plan as the best time to take it.

Information Literacy for Juniors at the University of Rhode Island

At this point in time, most of the information literacy instruction we provide at the junior (and senior) levels are subject-specific instruction sessions. Although we offer many sessions to students in a wide variety of disciplines, we are still formalizing the use of information literacy competencies within these instruction sessions. Our plan calls for us to provide this and other types of instruction. We have thought about our overall goal for this level but have not completed our work in this area.

In the junior year at URI, students begin course work in their declared major. We have found that this is a great time for them to intensify their knowledge of subject-specific information and the tools that help them find it. To capitalize on this situation we have planned for a modular and departmental approach to providing instruction to juniors.

IL in Action @ URI

Junior Year

In their junior year, students' course work becomes more subject-specific as most of the courses they take are in their major area of study. By the end of their junior year, students will have strengthened their mastery of introductory and advanced concepts and will have had extensive experience working with subject concepts and resources.

Information literacy in the junior year will be delivered primarily through the use of integrated instructional modules. Library faculty will collaborate with faculty members teaching courses in the students' major areas of study to design assignments, exercises, and instruction that emphasize subject-specific concepts and resources.

LIB 140: Special Topics in Information Literacy

Another option for the delivery of subject concepts is LIB 140. Junior-year students may opt to take this course, which will offer students in-depth opportunities to learn about information organization and resources in a specific field of study.

We are creating what we term "information literacy modules." These are conceived as "standardized toolboxes" geared to specific fields of study or topics, for example, "the professional and scholarly literature of engineering" or "company information." In our framework, each toolbox would contain concepts such as keyword versus subject searching or the "taxonomy of periodicals," skills such as how to evaluate the credibility of Web sites or how to locate a periodical article in the library, information resources, handouts, active-learning exercises, assignments, and so forth.

Modules will be developed for various subject areas, and will be designed to be sequential and cumulative in nature. They will be delivered in a number of different ways, as the course content requires. We envision that information literacy modules will be integrated with specific courses in the curriculum and incorporated into the final grades of the courses to which they are connected. This will necessarily require the cooperation of the regular classroom instructor. We plan to make the modules flexible so they will fit comfortably into the coursework. Our strategy is to create modules in several different formats so they can be delivered in person by the librarian or by the instructor, or they can be assigned as work to be done by the students outside of class.

We hope that once the modules find their appropriate place in the curriculum, they will continue an independent existence. This would be in contrast to our current model of subject-specific, one-shot library instruction sessions that depend on the motivation of classroom instructors to initiate and on specific assignments for topics covered.

Information Literacy for Seniors at the University of Rhode Island

During their senior year, students must complete a "capstone" project, which is meant to demonstrate mastery in their major area of study as well as the basic knowledge and research skills that should be achieved in earning a bachelor's degree. If the university's goals for graduates have been achieved, these capstone projects should show that to great effect. Our plan calls for an information literacy component to be attached to each of these capstone projects. Students will demonstrate their mastery of information literacy as it applies to each project. This might involve including an annotated bibliography that speaks to the selection and quality of sources used in the project. In a capstone project that relies on in-person interviews, demonstration of mastery might involve descriptions of "informants" and their qualifications to act as experts for the capstone project. As every capstone project has a research component, it will be fairly easy to incorporate assessment of the research component as the information literacy segment of the capstone project.

IL in Action @ URI

Economics majors at URI are required to take a three-credit course in their final semester. In the course, they complete a senior research project. In groups, students work collaboratively under the guidance of an economics faculty member and conduct in-depth research on the economic aspects of a topic of interest. At the end of the semester, they submit a written report and present their research in front of the class and the entire economics faculty.

Past research topics include the Chinese-U.S. exchange rate and its effect on economic activity in the United States, the effect of the minimum wage on poverty, comparing deregulation in the airline industry before and after 9/11, and the economics of a health care program in Rhode Island called RITe Aid and RITe Care aimed at those who cannot afford health insurance.

The business and economics librarian usually meets with this class to help them with their research. Prior to meeting with them, she gets a list of the group's projects from the faculty member teaching the class, which allows her to prepare lists of potential information sources for each group. As there are only four or five groups each semester, this is not an unreasonable amount of preparation. When she meets the class, she demonstrates information sources useful to all of them, such as the databases EconLit and ABI/INFORM. She also shows examples of information sources that might be important to specific groups, for example, the Bureau of Labor Statistics Web site. Throughout the semester, students are encouraged to e-mail the librarian for additional assistance if needed.

By the time students have completed their senior year of study, they should have mastered both basic and advanced concepts. They should have worked extensively with subject-specific resources and concepts in their fields and should be competent in applying universal concepts.

One method of demonstrating mastery of these concepts is through an information literacy portfolio project. In order to measure student outcomes in this area, we envision the portfolio project as part of the capstone course for departments and programs committed to information literacy.

IL in Action @ URI

Information Literacy Portfolio Project/Capstone Project

Departments and programs on campus will be encouraged to integrate information literacy competencies into student capstone projects. Librarians will provide assistance in the form of guidelines and assessment tools.

- Portfolio projects should be associated with a senior level course, preferably the capstone course in the declared major (e.g., Management 410).
- Portfolios will be used for assessment and evaluation of the effort, progress, and achievement of the student as well as the information literacy program.
- Portfolio projects will be a collection of student work that illustrates efforts, progress, and achievement of the information literate student.
- Portfolios may be print or electronic.
- Librarians will design the information literacy portfolio project guide for students and a portfolio assessment guide to assist teaching faculty in evaluation.

Library faculty will offer guidance to departments and programs in developing portfolio projects.

Another option for evaluating seniors' mastery of the information literacy concepts is the development and administration of a comprehensive examination in information literacy.

Information Literacy for Graduate Students at the University of Rhode Island

It is clear to those of us who work with graduate students that they may not have information literacy skills when they begin their graduate-level programs. Many of today's graduate students are returning to education after several years in the working world. Others continue directly from their undergraduate institutions. The level and comprehensiveness of

---

IL in Action @ URI

In spring 2000, the University of Rhode Island's Labor Research Center redesigned their master of science in labor relations and human resources curriculum. The faculty eliminated a previously required course on information sources and uses in labor relations and labor economics. While they did not feel that a full three-credit course in information skills was necessary, they recognized the importance of their graduates having the skills to access the literature of the field, to find labor and economic statistics, and to trace legislation. To that end, Professor Matthew Bodah, who previously taught the required course, contacted the business and government publications librarians, the two library faculty who had previously provided instruction for the information sources class. He suggested that together they develop a series of stand-alone library instruction sessions for LRC students.

The librarians proposed a series of modules, or one-to-two-hour instruction sessions that would be "connected" to specific courses in the master's curriculum. The modules would consist of instruction by a librarian or labor relations faculty member and/or Web-based tutorials covering specific topics.

Some of the suggested module topics were almost identical to what had been previously offered in "one-shot" bibliographic instruction sessions. The difference, however, was that the modules would be integrated into the curriculum as essential components of the program.

The labor relations and library faculty agreed on four module topics and the courses they would be connected to. Thus far, the first two modules have been designed and delivered in connection with LRS 500 Labor Relations and Human Resources, an introductory, graduate-level course.

The first module includes a tour of the library and a description of library services, an introduction to the library catalog, an in-class exercise on Library of Congress subject headings, and an assignment to create an annotated bibliography of five books on one of a number of suggested LR/HR topics.

In the second module, students are introduced to the different types of periodicals relevant to the field: news and popular press, professional/practitioner periodicals, and scholarly research journals. Students are then lead in a hands-on exploration and explanation of periodical databases such as ABI/INFORM, ERIC, PsycINFO, PAIS, and EconLit. Their assignment is to identify ten articles relevant to their topics using different databases. They document their search strategies and briefly describe the databases they use and the types of articles they are able to find in each one. According to the instructor of the course, student feedback after the modules is very positive. Students in the class who were not in the LR/HR program have commented that similar instruction should be part of every degree program.

IL in Action

Graduate Students

Some graduate students arrive direct from their undergraduate studies; others may have taken time out for work or family and are just returning to school. All graduate students are beginning a new level of research that is far more sophisticated than they have previously experienced.

To prepare these students we recommend:

- Seminars in subject-specific research processes
- Half-day programs, possibly during graduate school orientation at the beginning of each academic year or semester

IL in Action

Carol Ansel from Pine Point School in Stonington, Connecticut, has created a tiered system of instruction in her K-6 curriculum. She provides instruction to students as they become developmentally ready to learn each skill. For example, kindergarteners learn listening skills and basic library procedures like selecting books, checking them out, and taking care of them. The second graders learn about encyclopedias, the difference between fiction and nonfiction, and how to use the online catalog. By the time they reach sixth grade, students are ready to use the online catalog, periodical indexes, and Web searching to complete a research project.

information literacy instruction that graduate students have had when they enter graduate school is very uneven. Some will need a refresher course, others will need to start at the beginning, and others might need not need any instruction at all.

To level the playing field and allow graduate students to begin their programs armed with the tools and concepts they need to be successful, our plan offers a six-week, seminar-level class for graduate students. This class can be offered in specific disciplines, or it can be a more general class, incorporating students from many different disciplines. We have also proposed a half-day or full-day session that can be offered during the orientation program for new students. Our plan is flexible, designed to suit the needs of busy graduate students. Because these students are likely to be the teachers of future students, this is a very important group to target. If new faculty are already conversant with information literacy and its importance, it will not be difficult to convince them to support a program of information literacy.

Our plan specifies targets or goals for what students should know at any given time in their college careers. To accompany the plans for what instruction will be offered to students, we also crafted a plan for implementation of the pieces of the instruction puzzle. This strategy is an important part of the body of the plan, as it shows our readers that we have examined the reality of current practice and determined where our new practices could be inserted with most benefit to both students and instructors.

3.2.2 DIVIDE YOUR PLAN BY IMPLEMENTATION OF INSTRUCTION TO TARGET POPULATIONS

Once the parts of the plan become clear and you know what they will contain, you must think about how and when each part will be implemented. You may want to target certain classes to include information literacy modules or you may want to address the information literacy needs of one group of students at a time. Whatever your plan, you will want to spell out the details of how you will put your plan in place and then think about the work that involves. If you want to put an information literacy module into all "Introduction to Writing" courses, it will not happen by magic, but rather by contacting the writing department, discussing your ideas, convincing instructors that the addition of your module is a good thing, working with instructors to create a module specific to the needs of the class, and incorporating the module in the appropriate place(s) in the syllabus. Only then will you be ready to actually deliver this part of your plan.

This process will be important for each piece of your plan. Be generous in estimating how much time implementation will take. Even in the best of circumstances, implementation is not instantaneous.

IL in Action @ URI

URI is a medium-sized public research and graduate institution with a healthy undergraduate program. As such, we saw the need to create a plan that would answer the information literacy needs of students and faculty at many levels. We identified the introductory college programs as well as the largest colleges as places where the need was greatest. This group obviously needed general and across-the-board information.

We agreed that specialized sessions would be useful to students who had already declared a major. Students in the business program, for example, do not really use the library for business-related assignments until they have declared business as their major. This population would need more subject-specific programming.

Graduate students were also identified as needing instruction in information literacy, not only in terms of available tools, but which tools are the best to use in their specific discipline.

We thought that faculty might benefit from education and training in information literacy as well. Faculty may not be aware how much the library and the tools used in doing research have changed in the last decade. New faculty might not know what resources are available or which resources might support the classes they teach.

3.2.3 DIVIDE YOUR PLAN INTO SECTIONS BY DISCIPLINE OR PROGRAM

Many libraries have a liaison program with the departments of a college or university campus. While the process varies from institution to institution, it is frequently the case that the library has a subject specialist who acts as a liaison to the college and/or department housing that subject. That librarian will frequently introduce new resources and reference tools to his/her assigned department and solicit faculty requests for library materials. It is the liaison's job to see that the library needs of the college or department are being met as far as it is possible to do so.

Some subject-specialist librarians have attempted to systematize delivery of information literacy by using the connections already established in the liaison program. These subject-specialist librarians know the literature of the subject area and can craft exercises, modules, and/or credit-bearing courses that target the subject-specific tools that students in the department will need to be successful in their research. As the faculty and administration of the department will know the library liaison, it may be just a small step to incorporating an information literacy component into appropriate classes offered by the department.

It is also possible for any librarian to insert information literacy into individual departmental curricula by working with faculty in that area. This is as true for school librarians as it is for university librarians. Most instructors are willing to try out ideas that will make their work easier. One has only to show the increased quality of the work produced to convince those who have to evaluate the work that information literacy instruction will make their jobs easier.

IL in Action @ URI

Writing is a mandatory part of the University of Rhode Island's General Education program. Most University of Rhode Island students take Writing 104, "Writing to Inform and Explain," Writing 105, "Forms of College Writing," or Writing 106, "Writing from Field Print and Electronic Sources." Within this framework, the library's coordinator for the writing instruction program worked with the director of the college writing program to tailor the information literacy components of each course to the course's goals. WRT 104 students must identify their information needs and locate information, WRT 105 students must learn to select appropriate databases depending on their research area, and WRT 106 students learn to critically interact with information from a variety of sources such as primary texts, conversations with experts, journal articles, and the Web.

IL in Action

At Pine Point School in Stonington, Connecticut, the fourth graders work on a basic research report on animals. They use encyclopedias and books as sources. Librarian Carol Ansel instructs them in the use of these sources. At the fifth grade level, students do a more in-depth research report, requiring the use of books and journal articles. At this level, Ms. Ansel introduces them to online journal databases, search strategies, and basic methods of citation. In sixth grade, the students do a full blown research paper on birds. This paper requires the use of books, journal articles, and Web sites. Library instruction to accompany this project includes refresher information on finding books and searching for journal articles. In addition, students learn about Boolean searching as well as strategies for finding and evaluating information on the Web. Ansel has tailored the depth of instruction to match the needs of the students based on the complexity of the project they have been assigned.

It is necessary to identify specific courses for which information literacy instruction will be effective. We have found, for example, that most mathematics classes in algebra, geometry, calculus, and so on, have little scope for the inclusion of information literacy because library research is not required in the course. The course content simply does not lend itself to incorporation of information-literacy skills and concepts. Often, there is no requirement involving research and/or retrieval of information. However, *applied* statistics classes are another matter, as the application aspect of the course may require finding statistics of various kinds in business, government, or on the Internet.

Librarians must work with faculty to decide which competencies will be taught in which courses. Instead of meeting with certain classes on an ad hoc basis based on faculty-librarian relationships or faculty fondness for the library, incorporate into your plan a systematized approach to each department's curriculum that provides students with the information they need in the setting and at the time they need it.

Assessing your users' programmatic needs will help you succeed. Your needs assessment will tell you how many levels of instruction are needed. Thinking about the progress of students through their degrees will also help you determine when they should receive instruction. A first-year music student may have no need to use the library during that year, as performance may be the focus for beginning students. A first-year English student may need to know how to use the library right away. A professional school may need more instruction in the use of specific types of information, rather than a general approach. Design your program so that you will reach the students when the information is relevant to them.

3.2.4 DIVIDE YOUR PLAN INTO SECTIONS BY LOCATION OF INSTRUCTION

If you plan to deliver your information literacy program in multiple locations, one option might be to organize your plan on that basis. You may want to list instruction that will be delivered face-to-face separately from that which is mediated technologically. Face-to-face instruction might take place in a variety of settings, for example, in the library, computer labs, or as guest lectures in classes outside the library.

When choosing where to offer instruction, consider the advantages and disadvantages of different locations. In the library, you will be familiar with the resources and technologies on hand. When teaching outside the library, you may encounter surprises—availability of technology might differ and library resources will not be on hand. Many professors and students, however, like it when the librarian comes to their class. It makes the visitor seem important and to some extent it makes the students feel "honored" that an expert made time to visit the class. In addition, if the librarian goes to the classroom, the students (and the professor) do not need to re-member to come to the library, or interrupt their preset schedule, and they can maintain the level of comfort and familiarity they have established in their classroom.

It is possible that some of your instruction will not be in person at all. You may wish to consider instruction that is delivered by technology. This may be synchronous, for example, streaming video, teleconferencing, or PictureTel, or asynchronous, such as course management technologies like Web CT or Blackboard.

The advantages of transmitting library instruction are many. One li-brary instruction session could be broadcast by streaming video or Picture-Tel to reach any number of classes. This approach saves travel time for everyone and eliminates the need for a space in which a large number of students can gather at one time. Feedback opportunities are built into most systems, so students have the opportunity to ask questions. Asynchronous technologies like Web CT and Blackboard allow people to work at their own pace based on their own schedules. These technologies offer maxi-mum flexibility for learners and only require the librarian to present the in-formation at one time. Since the feedback mechanisms built into this type of system are, for the most part, written, shy people are more likely to par-ticipate and ask questions. Asynchronous instruction places the burden for receiving the information on the student. Using this type of technology re-quires discipline, organization, and some hands-on practice with comput-ers. The benefit of spontaneous interaction in the classroom is, of course, lost when using this technology.

You may be delivering your library instruction at multiple locations, branches, or campuses. Keep in mind that you may be dealing with differ-ent types of students, for example, adult, continuing education students versus traditional college-age students. These populations may require dif-ferent instructional techniques and technologies. While using the same course materials in all locations eliminates the work of developing instruc-tional materials for each location, you may need to modify these materials based on your audience.

In addition to providing information literacy instruction to your pri-mary users, you may wish to consider whether to include in your plan those outside your institutional boundaries. Through presentations to student clubs, alumni organizations, and community groups such as investment clubs, scouting groups, 4-H, and Rotary clubs, you will garner broad-based sup-port as well as deliver lifelong learning skills to those who might not oth-erwise receive them.

IL in Action @ URI

URI has three separate and distinct campuses. Each has its own library and staff. Each serves a different type of stu-dent. To accommodate the va-riety of students at the three campuses, we use a variety of methods to bring appropriate levels of instruction to the ap-propriate location in the appro-priate time frame.

> **IL in Action @ URI**
>
> At URI, librarians have given presentations on information gathering skills and library resources to a wide variety of groups outside of the traditional classroom. The business librarian has provided instruction to local women's investment clubs and a community organization teaching people how to set up microbusinesses. Several library faculty have given library tours and talks to Boy Scouts and middle school and junior high school students. The science librarian has met with a student club in engineering to reach students who might not receive instruction through their engineering classes.

3.2.5 DIVIDE YOUR PLAN BY METHOD OF DELIVERY

To some extent, your method of delivery may be driven by the location where instruction takes place.

How many different ways will you reach students?

- Web tutorials/Online tutorials?
- Videos?
- Credit courses delivered in person or by distance education?
- Workshops?
- One-shot sessions?
- Seminars?
- Web CT classes?
- Web CT outreach/Integration with other classes?
- A workbook?

Do students work on homework at home? If so, your plan will need to address the technology needs of the students. Will they need access to computers? Is this the only way they can receive the information? Will students be expected to absorb instructional materials independently, or will a moderator or instructor be available to interpret and answer questions?

Match the content of the instruction to the delivery mode selected. For example, chunking text for online instruction makes reading and absorbing the information easier. Chunking refers to dividing a whole topic into smaller segments to make reading the information on as computer screen easier and more pleasant. A self-grading or interactive quiz following a Web-based asynchronous instruction session can provide the student with immediate feedback/correction.

Will you offer a for-credit course, workshops, or one-shot sessions? Will you offer in-depth information or gear your program to students at an introductory level? Pick the best combination of delivery modes for your students and situation. Not all delivery modes are desirable or indeed necessary for every situation. You are the best judge of what is needed and what new ideas would be useful. Keep in mind that you want to allow flex-

> **IL in Action**
>
> For integrated state systems or consortia that consist of a combination of universities, colleges, and community colleges different types of schools might work together on one program. In Rhode Island, the HELIN consortium consists of ten libraries from a variety of institutional types—public and private, large and small, two-year and four-year, undergraduate, and graduate. A Web tutorial is in development to teach information literacy skills to students from all of these institutions at a generalized level.

ibility and choice for students and instructors, but do not try to incorporate everything if half of it will never be useful.

3.2.6 DIVIDE YOUR PLAN INTO SECTIONS BY IMPLEMENTATION TIME FRAMES

In this case, you write the plan based on what ideas you can implement right away. Perhaps you can incorporate information-literacy concepts in all library instruction sessions for freshmen in the coming year. Using the time frame approach, you might make this the first part of the body of your plan.

You will then proceed to describe what you can accomplish in year two, three, and so on. This approach allows some time for additional resources to be acquired if necessary. It allows your program to grow gradually. The plan will clearly show proposed growth over time. When presenting a plan to administrators and boards, this approach may be the most comprehensible.

What part of the plan will you deliver first? What will follow? What can you accomplish right away with the resources you already have? What are reasonable goals for the upcoming year or two?

If you are creating a comprehensive plan for information literacy in a K-6 school, you might decide to start with the sixth grade program because those students are the ones who will be leaving your school first. This is also the group that will most benefit from the acquisition of information-literacy skills that will be used during their seventh grade experience. In year two of your plan, you may decide to add a plan for the fifth grade. In year three, you might add a new aspect of technology or bring in a program for younger students.

> ### IL in Action @ URI
>
> At URI, when we envisioned course offerings, we decided to plan and implement a credit course for undergraduates first. From there, we decided to create subject-specific modules that could be applied at the appropriate time after students declared their majors. We then planned a Web-based tutorial to assist in providing very basic instruction to large numbers of undergraduates. This was a plan for the near future. The next phase, a program for graduate students with attention to faculty needs to follow, was planned for the distant future.

The design of this part of the plan will be very important. You may want to try several layouts and/or approaches to get a visual impression of what they will look like. The approach or approaches you select must be explained as clearly and as succinctly as possible. We have listed some ideas about how to design the body of your plan below.

Instructions: Brainstorm ideas about how you could organize your plan and use the worksheet to jot down your ideas.

Divide into sections by student year in school:

_____

_____

_____

_____

Divide into sections by discipline or program:

_____

_____

_____

_____

Divide into sections by type of instruction:

_____

_____

_____

_____

Divide into sections by location of instruction:

_____

_____

_____

_____

Divide into sections by time frames (present, near future, distant future, and so on):

_____

_____

_____

_____

Worksheet 3-C. Design the Body of the Plan

3.3 IMPLEMENT A TIMETABLE

Even if you do not choose to describe your plan through implementation timelines, you will need to consider how long each part of your plan will take to put into place. This will in some measure be controlled by the number of people you have to work with, funding, available space, and the mandate(s) from your administration. A timeline will show your readers when to expect each part of your plan to become a reality. Try to estimate reasonable completion dates for all parts of your plan. (Remember that your plan is a dynamic document and can be updated and changed if you finish something early or find that you have not allowed enough time for something.)

Make a to-do list and consider how long each task will take to accomplish. Consider how many people you have available and how many tasks can be accomplished at the same time.

3.4 LAUNCH THE APPROVAL PROCESSES

3.4.1 GETTING APPROVAL FOR THE PLAN ITSELF

Approvals can take time. The bigger the idea, the more time it will take to get it approved. To get approval for a comprehensive plan for an entire institution, you may have to get the okay from multiple levels and several different groups. You will need to know who approves plans of this type at your institution. You will also need to know when approvals take place. Many institutions approve new programs on a cyclical schedule so revision and/or implementation can take place in a timely manner.

3.4.2 ACQUIRING APPROVAL FOR NEW COURSES

Can a new course get through the approval process in one to two years? If you intend to introduce new courses, make sure you know the procedure, how long it will take, and what the important deadlines are.

> **IL in Action @ URI**
>
> At URI, we submitted our plan to the various decision-making bodies of the library and then revised our document based on their input. As a result, there were thirteen revisions of our plan before the final version was approved, two years after the first version was discussed.

> **IL in Action @ URI**
>
> At URI, the course approval process is very regimented. It requires the approval of several different bodies, all of which meet at different times. So planning our timing to make sure our course was discussed at the appropriate level at the appropriate time was very important.

IL in Action @ URI

As a part of the government of the State of Rhode Island, the workings of the university, such as hiring and the creation of positions, are controlled outside of the university. This is a time consuming and political process. Also, as a small state, finding the money to pay for everything we hope to do is not an easy task. Therefore, we did not make any part of our plan dependent on new positions. There was no guarantee that we would be able to get them, and we were eager to put the first pieces of our plan in place. We decided to work with the materials already available to us. When it became clear, however, that more sections of our course were needed, a mechanism was invented to provide the faculty to teach them. We hired several people at the per-course instructor level, as if they were to teach the course. Instead, those new people staffed the reference desk, releasing the library faculty members to teach. This allowed us to add more staff without creating any permanent positions.

3.4.3 GETTING APPROVAL FOR FUNDING NEW POSITIONS

If the success of your plan depends on creating new positions, how long will it take to get those new positions? If you have a mandate to make your information-literacy program a reality, money may already be available and positions may be waiting to be filled. Some institutions have the latitude to make swift decisions regarding the creation of positions and allocation of funds. Other institutions have a much more convoluted process that requires time, signatures, and political influence. Make sure you know what the process is at your institution and how to make it work for you.

3.4.2 GETTING APPROVAL FOR NEW TECHNOLOGY AND CLASSROOM EQUIPMENT

Will your program require the acquisition of new technology and classroom equipment? What is the budgeting process and the timeframe for making requests and receiving new equipment? Can you make your program work with incremental additions or will you need to have everything at the same time?

If you hope to write and receive a grant for equipment, you will need to investigate the timelines for each specific grant you write. No two are the same and rarely do the timelines for any two grants coincide.

IL in Action @ URI

At URI, the steps taken to get our plan approved became so numerous we decided to make a chart to show what our experience was like.

Information Literacy "Timeline" at the University of Rhode Island

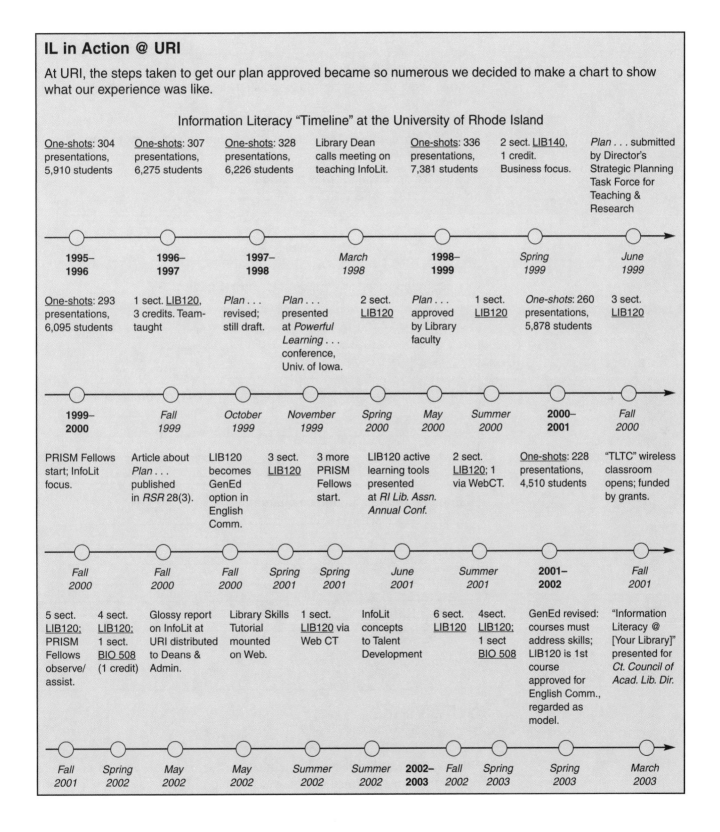

One-shots: 304 presentations, 5,910 students | One-shots: 307 presentations, 6,275 students | One-shots: 328 presentations, 6,226 students | Library Dean calls meeting on teaching InfoLit. | One-shots: 336 presentations, 7,381 students | 2 sect. LIB140, 1 credit. Business focus. | Plan . . . submitted by Director's Strategic Planning Task Force for Teaching & Research

1995–1996 | **1996–1997** | **1997–1998** | March 1998 | **1998–1999** | Spring 1999 | June 1999

One-shots: 293 presentations, 6,095 students | 1 sect. LIB120, 3 credits. Team-taught | Plan . . . revised; still draft. | Plan . . . presented at Powerful Learning . . . conference, Univ. of Iowa. | 2 sect. LIB120 | Plan . . . approved by Library faculty | 1 sect. LIB120 | One-shots: 260 presentations, 5,878 students | 3 sect. LIB120

1999–2000 | Fall 1999 | October 1999 | November 1999 | Spring 2000 | May 2000 | Summer 2000 | **2000–2001** | Fall 2000

PRISM Fellows start; InfoLit focus. | Article about Plan . . . published in RSR 28(3). | LIB120 becomes GenEd option in English Comm. | 3 sect. LIB120 | 3 more PRISM Fellows start. | LIB120 active learning tools presented at RI Lib. Assn. Annual Conf. | 2 sect. LIB120; 1 via WebCT. | One-shots: 228 presentations, 4,510 students | "TLTC" wireless classroom opens; funded by grants.

Fall 2000 | Fall 2000 | Fall 2000 | Spring 2001 | Spring 2001 | June 2001 | Summer 2001 | **2001–2002** | Fall 2001

5 sect. LIB120; PRISM Fellows observe/ assist. | 4 sect. LIB120; 1 sect. BIO 508 (1 credit) | Glossy report on InfoLit at URI distributed to Deans & Admin. | Library Skills Tutorial mounted on Web. | 1 sect. LIB120 via Web CT | InfoLit concepts to Talent Development | 6 sect. LIB120 | 4sect. LIB120; 1 sect BIO 508 | GenEd revised: courses must address skills; LIB120 is 1st course approved for English Comm., regarded as model. | "Information Literacy @ [Your Library]" presented for Ct. Council of Acad. Lib. Dir.

Fall 2001 | Spring 2002 | May 2002 | May 2002 | Summer 2002 | Summer 2002 | **2002–2003** | Fall 2002 | Spring 2003 | Spring 2003 | March 2003

Which parts of the plan do you want to achieve in the not-too-distant future? Which parts will you establish later? Below are some ideas about what might be accomplished in the short-term time frame that you choose.

Instructions: Brainstorm about timetables you must meet and note them below.

Acquire approval for new courses:

_____
_____
_____
_____

Acquire approval and funding for new positions:

_____
_____
_____
_____

Acquire approval for new technology and classroom equipment:

_____
_____
_____
_____

Educate Your institution's community:

_____
_____
_____
_____

Worksheet 3-D. Establish Realistic Timetables

SUMMARY

When you have decided what elements to include in your plan and have placed them in a document that is visually pleasing and easy to understand, the hardest part of your job is complete. There may be many revisions, but these will be minor compared with what you have accomplished up to this point.

ASSESS, MAINTAIN, AND PROMOTE THE PLAN

YOUR PLAN

You must have mechanisms in place to keep your plan moving forward, to determine how well it is meeting its goals, and to let all parties concerned know how well you are doing. The details for how all this will happen should be explained in your plan.

4.1 ESTABLISH OVERSIGHT FOR THE PLAN

The people in the information literacy planning group and the writing group already may be potential members of the group that eventually could be responsible for oversight of your information literacy plan and program. The oversight group could be broad based, representing a number of constituencies from your institution, or it could be composed primarily of staff from your library.

Before you decide on your oversight group, check for any mandates, rules, regulations, or existing committee structures at the library, institution, school district, or state level. Check for an oversight group that might already exist. Check for mandates. Does your program have to be directed by your school district, principal, or accreditation agency? If so you must abide by the rules already in place for oversight. Do not break rules or step on toes where mandates or past practices have already established oversight responsibilities. This is where doing your homework will save you time and effort. If oversight has already been addressed, do not try to change it—at least not through your plan.

If you can develop your own plan for oversight, do so. If you cannot develop one, try to work your way in so that those involved most closely with the plan/program have some direct input into its oversight. Those people most actively involved in the program will have a vested interest in its success and will know intimately what goes wrong or what does not work well.

Keep in mind that some oversight bodies are made up of people who do not have any direct experience with information literacy per se. A committee of this type might be advisory only. Learn what you can about the group that will oversee your program. The group may or may not have been granted any power. Knowing what their authority is will be very helpful in determining how you will craft your plans and your document.

There are a number of advantages of a broad-based oversight group. Not only will such a group provide many fresh ideas and points of view, but having people from outside the library will create interest in the community by those who are members of the oversight group. By interacting with people working in other parts of your institution, you are more likely to hear about changes, initiatives, and upcoming events occurring in other parts of the community, for example, upcoming accreditations, state-level mandates, new programs and courses, and so on. By working with people from outside your own institution you can learn about opportunities and applications, funding sources, and community grants you might otherwise not find. In general, more information will flow in all directions. You might be able to tap new sources of funding by using a broad-based group.

Of course, a broad-based group may have disadvantages as well. The library will not have as much control over the plan, its programs, and/or the implementation. You may be subject to political infighting, wrestling for limited funds, staff, space, or attention. People serving on a broad-based oversight committee might not have adequate time or level of interest to devote to the program.

Small oversight groups tend to be made up of those more closely involved with the daily operations of any program or project. Members tend to come from places closer to the center of the program. You might expect a small oversight group to include someone who is involved with delivery of each segment of the plan; someone who has the power to make decisions regarding funding, staffing, space, and so on; someone from outside the library who might be involved as a partner or whose work might be affected by the plan; and someone who can market the plan.

It is very important to explain in detail who will be in charge and who will bear responsibility for the plan. If the program is an orphan in your organization, there will be no mechanism for its care and feeding, no avenue by which it can be launched, and no viable way to assess its success or failure.

In your plan, be sure to explain who will administer your program. If the library is to "own" the program, it will be administered by the library. If you are partnering with another department or departments on campus, explain who will be in charge and who will bear the responsibility for the program. If the school district or the state Department of Education will administer the program, make sure that their responsibilities are clearly spelled out in your plan.

IL in Action

At Pine Point School in Stonington, Connecticut, oversight of the information literacy plan is the responsibility of the librarian, in consultation with the faculty. Librarian Carol Ansel assesses the success of her curriculum by reviewing fourth through sixth grade reports. If problem areas become apparent, she adjusts her teaching methods, her examples, or the amount of time spent on instruction in that area.

4.2 CONSTRUCT ASSESSMENT STRATEGIES

Perhaps the most difficult part of creating a comprehensive plan for information literacy is deciding how you will measure your progress and success. Assessment results are a big part of what administrators will use to determine the success or failure of your program.

Measuring success can be a difficult task. Knowing what to measure and how to measure will require careful thought. Fortunately, assessment is now at the forefront of education and library planning. Accrediting agencies, educational governing bodies, and professional organizations are very much interested in finding out how they can show that the outcome of their efforts is positive and that the students who receive instruction finish with the knowledge they will need to be lifelong learners.

There are many problems with assessment. It is often difficult to measure what or how much an individual has learned. It is difficult to craft measurements that are precise and informative. For example, it is easy to count the number of students who received library instruction during a specified time period. It is difficult to determine, however, what they learned and it is even more difficult to find out how long the information was retained.

There are two basic types of assessment. The first is quantitative. Quantitative assessment provides information through statistics. In some cases, simple statistics or quantitative information will be useful and provide basic information about your programs. The second type of assessment is qualitative. It is descriptive in nature and results from in-person interviews, written answers to open-ended questions or observed actions. In some cases, qualitative information from individuals may be more useful and informative. Combinations of different kinds of assessments will probably be needed to present the holistic picture of how well your plan and its programs are working. In your information literacy plan utilize a variety of approaches, both broad and narrow.

Course Evaluation

Pre- and posttests, questionnaires, or surveys can be implemented in either print or electronic formats to evaluate a short course, credit course, or online course or module. Both student satisfaction surveys and learning outcomes tests will provide useful information.

IL in Action @ URI

At URI, we worked with Bette Erickson, one of the instructional development experts on our campus, to develop a student satisfaction survey about our credit-bearing information literacy course. All sections of the course distribute the survey to their students. The anonymous surveys are gathered by a member of the class and mailed to the IDP office where they are analyzed. After the semester ends, we receive the results. When we began teaching the course we wanted to know if students found the course effective and useful. After several years, we revised the survey, dropping some questions and adding others. These surveys are very useful to the LIB 120 instruction team because they include questions specific to the course content and written comments from the students regarding the value of the course to their research skills.

Student Learning Outcomes

Student learning can be assessed using traditional techniques such as surveys, worksheets, quizzes, tests, and individual course assignments. Other methods, such as the Minute Paper (a brief essay demonstrating that the student has understood the material), the Muddiest Point (an opportunity for students to identify and clarify anything they did not understand), and simply asking for a one-sentence summary are also very useful. Research projects that result in written works such as papers, portfolios, and/or annotated bibliographies generally provide a good indication of a student's learning of information literacy competencies. Other ideas include presentations of research results to the class using a Web site or Power Point presentation that they have designed to display and illustrate the information.

Look to the Center for Teaching Excellence or instructional development staff for help with designing assessment and evaluation tools. Many institutions have instructor teaching evaluation programs already in place. You may be able to utilize these assessment tools or revise them to fit your needs. You may find other assessment and evaluation tools such as print, automated, and Web-based surveys on many library instruction Web sites and in books on information literacy. You may plan to have instructors of your information literacy program attend the Association of College and Research Libraries' Immersion Program. This program is an intensive, four-and-a-half-day program focusing on all aspects of designing and delivering an information literacy program.

Individual components of your program can be assessed with traditional tools. Pre- and posttests are useful gauges for the immediate outcomes of instructional sessions and credit courses. The instruments used to measure what has been learned should be carefully crafted to show both proficiency in skills and concepts. You may be able to use an instrument created by someone else, or you may want to create your own. No matter which you choose, keep in mind what you want to measure. Make sure that the type of instrument you use and the questions you ask will supply you with the measurement you are seeking.

Practical applications can also be used to measure student learning. Students might be asked to complete a task or tasks. For example, if your teaching goal is to teach students how to find a book using the online catalog, each student should be required to find a book in the online catalog using information supplied (author, title, keyword, and so on). Students' achievements in completing different tasks will show the success of the teaching strategy and the level of learning received. Tests, presentations, portfolios, and projects can all be used to measure the learning outcomes for individual tasks, entire modules, or credit-bearing classes. This type of assessment can be done at any level, and for any grade.

Overall student learning and mastery could be measured with a capstone project. A capstone or final project required of students finishing a particular grade level, completing high school, or at the college level, can be crafted specifically to address information literacy, or could be combined with other graduation requirements. For example, some colleges require students to create a portfolio of projects they have completed during their college education that shows what they have learned. Part of the assessment of the portfolio could relate to information literacy skills demonstrated in the contents of the portfolio. Some high schools require students to write a senior thesis as a graduation requirement. This is a more traditional assignment and the information literacy component could be assessed by the strength of the bibliography and the quality of the information selected. Some schools, colleges, and universities require students to pass an information or library skills test as a graduation requirement. This is often a stand-alone set of tasks demonstrating research and evaluation skills and understanding of the underlying concepts.

Overall Program Performance

To assess the overall success of a program similar strategies might be used, but the information sought will target not the individual student, but the success or failure of the means by which those students are taught. Statistics from the assessment of individual levels of learning could be compiled to see the larger picture about the whole program. Gather those statistics. In addition, look at the whole program and ask questions about its efficacy. This can be done in a variety of ways using surveys, analysis of grades, or analysis of portfolio or capstone project results.

IL in Action

Project Sails is a standardized instrument developed at Kent State University.

The purpose of the Project for Standardized Assessment of Information Literacy Skills (SAILS) has been to develop an instrument for programmatic level assessment of information literacy skills that is valid and thus credible to university administrators and other academic personnel. We envisioned a tool to measure information literacy that:

- Is standardized
- Contains items not specific to a particular institution or library
- Is easily administered
- Has been proven valid and reliable
- Assesses at institutional level
- Provides for both external and internal benchmarking

This formal survey has been designed and tested from 2002 to 2004 specifically for assessment of information literacy programs.

Source: sails.lms.kent.edu/ index.php

Instructor Teaching Evaluation

There are both formal and informal methods for evaluating individual instructor classroom teaching. Informal evaluation can be done through peer or mentor observations that utilize checklists, rating scales, and written or verbal feedback of the teaching experience.

Many institutions of higher education have university-wide teaching or course evaluation programs. At URI, we use the Student Evaluation of Teaching (SET) process, which gives students an opportunity to anonymously evaluate different aspects of teaching performance including instructor evaluation and course design. The results are received by instructors several months after the SET is distributed. Instructors may use these to review their teaching methods as well as including the results as documentation for annual performance reviews. These evaluations can be useful, but often they do not generate meaningful summative information for instructors.

More formal assessment can be accomplished through commercially designed or externally produced surveys or those designed in-house. ALA and its divisions have links to a large number of useful documents concerning assessment. For example, AASL has an assessment bibliography at their Web site, www.ala.org/ala/aasl/aaslproftools/informationpower/information power.htm. ACRL's effective practices site has a page on assessment issues, www.ala.org/ala/acrl/acrlissues/acrlinfolit/infolitresources/infolitassess /assessmentissues.htm, as well as a page of bibliographies on assessments of various types (www.ala.org/ala/acrlbucket/infolit/bibliographies1/assess-mentbibliography.htm). By using the appropriate instrument, you can be specific and comprehensive in your approach to assessment.

Programatic assessment is usually done by the oversight group for the plan, which should include one or more mechanisms for providing assessment of individual parts of the plan and for the plan as a whole. Assessment is an ongoing task. Your oversight group must be given a specific charge that will promote the accomplishment of the various kinds of assessment that will best serve you, your plan, your institution, and your students.

Spell out who is responsible for the care and feeding of your plan. Make sure you think about how and when you will assess the progress of your plan in part and as a whole. We have listed some topics you might want to address in this part of your plan.

Instructions: Brainstorm ideas about oversight and assessment suited to your institution and write them down below.

Establish an oversight committee for the plan and program:

_____

_____

_____

_____

Establish program assessment tools:

_____

_____

_____

_____

Create a timetable for assessment of parts of the plan and for the plan as a whole:

_____

_____

_____

_____

Create a timetable for reporting the results of your assessments:

_____

_____

_____

_____

Worksheet 4-A. Institute Oversight and Assessment Procedures

4.3 MARKET THE PLAN USING PUBLIC RELATIONS

How will you tell people about your plan? Once it exists, sharing it with as many people as possible should be a goal. You must determine with whom you want to share it and how to put it in their hands. Think outside the box. Of course you want your students, faculty, and administrators to know. What about alumni, the board of governors, local employers, college recruiters, prospective students and their parents, or other libraries?

Once approved, be sure to inform all interested parties about the plan. Send the appropriate versions of the proposed plan to the appropriate groups. Post it prominently on your Web page. Send copies out by e-mail. Send paper copies. Write a story for the student newspaper. Announce the plan in the faculty newsletters and departmental meetings. Have library liaisons meet with their departments to discuss the plan. Make sure people know and remember that your plan is in place.

4.3.1 GET YOUR PLAN APPROVED OR ENDORSED BY THE INSTITUTIONAL DECISION MAKERS

There are numerous ways to provide institutional decision makers with information about your plan. If you can get any group of decision makers to approve or endorse your plan, formally or informally, you can use that endorsement to market your plan to others.

4.3.2 SCHOOL BOARDS, REGIONAL SCHOOL DISTRICTS, STATE DEPARTMENTS OF EDUCATION

It may be that your local school board or a larger administrative organization would appreciate a report about your plan. It will be to your advantage to explain your plan and what it will do for your students. There is usually a mechanism that will allow you to make presentations to these groups. It may be a simple telephone call to a secretary asking that you be put on the next agenda, or it may be a more formal process.

4.3.3 MARKET YOUR PLAN TO THE LIBRARY PROFESSION

There are many opportunities for librarians to promote and market their plan within the profession. By placing your plan on your library's Web site

---

IL in Action @ URI

At URI, we arranged to make a presentation to the council of deans concerning our plan for information literacy and our 3-credit course. The council is made up of the deans of each college at the university. It meets on a regular basis to discuss plans for the future, to inform each other of new programs and initiatives, and to grapple with budget and personnel issues. We decided that making a presentation to this group would be a valuable means of marketing our new plan and our new course.

you make it accessible to others. When other institutions are looking for models to consider, a quick search of the Web will turn up your plan.

You can send your plan to ERIC (Educational Resources Information Center). This organization houses files of education-related materials and is one of the major providers of education-related information, including journal articles, reports, curricula plans, and more. ERIC indexes education-related materials so they can be located by researchers. This is another way your plan can be made public and accessible.

Publishing articles is a great way to market your plan. You might have a local newsletter for librarians in your library or in your region. Your parent/teacher organization may have a newsletter, Web site, or other publication. There are many professional and research journals in librarianship that publish a wide range of information. Getting information about your plan out to other library professionals is a great way to gain recognition and to share your ideas.

Speak up. There are many opportunities to speak to groups. You might consider making a presentation at a teacher in-service meeting, a faculty meeting, and/or a PTO meeting. You might speak at a college advisors' meeting or a new faculty orientation. ALA, AASL, SLA, ACRL, LOEX, and many other organizations have regular meetings for the purpose of continuing education of librarians. Their conferences are perfect places to tell others about your plan.

4.3.4 MARKETING THE PROGRAM TO STUDENTS

You may want to consider and plan how you will get students to participate in your program. What will motivate them to participate? Can your plan be made an institutional requirement? Can students get credit or certification? Can you create some excitement and interest from future participants in your plan by doing something unexpected and/or novel?

You might design posters to describe and advertise your plan and the parts that will be of most interest to your students. To get more involvement you might ask students to participate in a contest to design those posters for you.

People love games and prizes. You might create an information literacy carnival for the week you announce your plan. You could set up booths with different activities at each: ask students to answer trivia questions, have participants guess information-literacy-related words, pop a balloon with a dart to win a prize, make fortune cookies with information-literacy-related fortunes inside. Think of all the carnivals you have ever been to and adapt the games to information-literacy advertising.

People love food. You might decide to sponsor an event that includes refreshments. Again, you might make it information-literacy related by creating questions about recipes, weights and measures, ingredients, chemistry, and so on.

IL in Action

At Roger Williams University in Bristol, Rhode Island, the library participated in the LibQUAL survey. In order to attract participants, the library staff created a lively and exciting marketing plan that targeted students and faculty to encourage them to fill out the online survey. They made posters and distributed them widely. They made bookmarks containing the dates the survey would be available and the URL necessary to get to the site. They got coupons for free coffee, bookstore items, and several enticing "grand prizes" from their local office supplier, which they gave away to students and faculty who participated in filling out the survey. They held a pizza party in the library, and asked everyone who attended to log on and fill out the survey. Their multifaceted marketing approach generated a good deal of interest and participation. This resulted in campuswide knowledge about the survey, new or renewed interest in the library, and a large number of respondents who completed the survey.

IL in Action @ URI

At URI, we created our three-credit course in information literacy to stand alone. It was not attached to any other course, nor was it required in any discipline. In order to create an incentive for students to take this course as an elective, we decided to look at the requirements for courses that fulfill the General Education requirements. This designation attracts students who want to complete their General Education requirements, and by doing so, students feel that they "get" something beyond the three credits and the course content.

By following the proper procedures, crafting our syllabus to demonstrate that the necessary elements for general education classification were included, and getting the necessary approvals, our course was listed as one that fulfills the general education requirement in the area of English communication. This provides students with an incentive for taking our course as opposed to some other course.

Everyone likes to get something for free. You might contact local eateries, bookstores, office supply companies, or clothing stores to ask for donations of small items that could be used for prizes and/or free giveaways. It provides advertising for the business and also promotes your information literacy cause as well.

4.3.5 MARKETING THE PROGRAM TO LIBRARY STAFF

Where will you get the people to deliver the program? Will you have to convince library staff or will they stand in line to volunteer? Will they need a pep rally or a dynamite charge to get them going? Will they agree to try something on a short-term basis with assessment to follow? Will they know how to provide essential information to students, faculty, parents, or others who inquire? Will they do the typing and/or photocopying? Once again, you want to emphasize the benefits of your plan from the perspective of the library staff. If it means more work for them, at least explain the benefits that an increased workload will have in the long run. There are many ways to market your plan to library staff. You may be able to offer release time for staff willing to spend time preparing for a class. You might be able to offer additional pay. You might be able to offer training that will make library staff more information literate. Perhaps you can offer prizes for the best IL class exercise or the first five people who volunteer to sign up for a workshop. A coveted parking space for a month? A gift certificate at the school bookstore? A tee shirt with a funny IL related inscription? Free pens or highlighters? There are many ways to generate excitement for new programs even if it means more work for the staff.

4.3.6 MARKETING THE PROGRAM TO FACULTY, STAFF, AND ADMINISTRATION

Telling these people about your program will be important. You will also want to tell them how your plan is going to make their lives better. How will it make their jobs easier? Will your plan help eliminate plagiarism in term papers? Will your plan help teach students to evaluate the quality of the materials they chose to use in their projects and presentations? Will your plan eliminate some of the work that the individual faculty, staff, and/or administration member has to do now?

IL in Action @ URI

At URI, librarians found many ways to get the word out about our plan and our program. We are all subject selectors and curriculum liaisons to individual departments. We are all representatives on various campus committees. These responsibilities offer endless opportunities for introducing information literacy to our colleagues. We used these opportunities in our marketing to that population. We also made personal contact with the faculty, from lunch dates to university functions. We made a presentation to the council of deans at one of their meetings and were overwhelmed by their enthusiastic response. You will need to get out and talk to people at your institution, at their convenience, about your plan.

You must let people know that you have a plan. You should let them know how your plan is going to make their lives better. You might want to tell them how their participation in your plan will give them an advantage over those who do not participate. We have suggested several categories of people to whom you may want to market your plan and some ideas about how to reach them.

Instructions: Brainstorm ideas about marketing, including who you will market to and what methods you will use.

Marketing the program to students (incentives: from general education credits to free candy bars):

_____

_____

_____

_____

Marketing the program to library staff (workshops, training sessions, brochures, rewards):

_____

_____

_____

_____

Marketing the program to faculty, staff, and administration (newsletters, departmental presentations, open house visits, one-on-one discussions, workshops):

_____

_____

_____

_____

Marketing the program to parents and the public (open house, newsletter, guest-speaker events):

_____

_____

_____

_____

Marketing the plan to funding agencies (grant proposals):

_____

_____

_____

_____

Worksheet 4-B. Make and Launch a Marketing Plan

4.4 CREATE PROGRESS REPORTS

Any program worth continuing must have a means of reinventing and renewing itself. There are many possible ways to evaluate what has been done so far and what needs to be done in the future.

4.4.1 ANNUAL REPORT

Undoubtedly, you will produce an annual report for your plan, including what you accomplished during the past year and how many people you served. Even if this report is not required, you can make it part of your plan. The annual report is a good way to document what has been accomplished and what still needs to be done. It will provide a mechanism for affirming the accuracy of your timetable or the need for its revision. Sometimes you get so caught up in the day-to-day tasks of providing instruction that you do not take the time to step back and look at the big picture of what has been accomplished in an academic year. Writing an annual report will supply the perspective needed to "back up" and look at the broad picture of how your information literacy plan fits into the larger landscape of your institution.

4.4.2 STATISTICS

It is always good to be able to quantify the results of your work. Somehow, numbers make projects seem more important. By simply counting (the number of people affected by the implementation of your plan; the number of hits on your Web-based, information-literacy tutorial; the number of bookmarks you handed out or posters you posted) you have some measure of what you have accomplished. By compiling or comparing these numbers over a period of time you will have some idea of how your plan is growing, shifting, and changing. Statistics can be used as benchmarks over a period of time and are certainly something you can point to when asked about the results of the implementation of your plan.

4.4.3 SPECIAL PUBLICATIONS

If you hope to get the attention of a particular audience or to keep them informed of your progress, you may want to create a special publication. In this type of document, you can tailor the information you want to deliver to the audience that will receive it.

IL in Action @ URI

At URI, we decided that it was appropriate to update the administration about what we had accomplished during the first years that our information literacy plan was in place. We created a document explaining what we were trying to accomplish and what we had done so far. This report contained understandable statistics presented with numbers and bar graphs. The document highlighted our successes and outlined what we wanted to do in the near future. It also indicated what we expected in the way of support from administrators in order to continue the implementation of our program. We sent this document to the administration of the university and the board of governors of the university.

4.4.4 ANNUAL PLANNING RETREAT TO PLAN THE NEXT OBJECTIVES

We have found it very helpful to return to the document on a regular basis, both to consider where we are and to determine what we need to do next. A retreat may focus on the implementation of new parts of the plan or review problems and successes of the past year, or it may be a combination of both. A retreat can also be a time to bring new people on board and/or to report to administrative bodies on your progress.

4.4.5 REVISIT AND ASSESS THE PROGRAM'S GOALS

Is it working? Are you getting where you meant to go? Do you need to address problems, fine tune first attempts or take a new direction? Are there new variables to consider? Assessments of this type will probably take place casually but should also occur in a formal way as well. You may gather your planning committee to address these questions. You might want to hold more open-space meetings, or create focus groups to react to specific parts of the plan. If the plan needs to be tweaked a little or changed a lot, you will need to find out by comparing the program's goals with the outcomes.

4.4.6 MARKET THE PLAN AND THE PROGRAM

As your plan takes shape and your program begins, it is important to inform and "sell" it to your audience. Make sure people hear about what you have done and how it benefits them. Once your reports are written, make sure they are broadcast to the widest possible audience. You could extract the statistics, for example, and provide them to your institution's research department if you have one. You could ask a reporter from the local newspaper to come and do a feature on your new program. This is the place to think outside the box and to use creative measures to market your hard work to the public.

4.4.7 REPORT THE SUCCESSES WIDELY

Even if reports are not required, there is nothing against creating one anyway. If reports must be official, then perhaps you could post a blog on your Web site, telling the story of your information literacy plan. You might want to create some kind of document or brochure you could give to parents to show how their children are benefiting from your plan and your programs.

> **IL in Action @ URI**
>
> At the end of the third year of our program, we created a report on our progress and sent it to the university president, provost and deans, as well as the board of governors for higher education. They did not ask us for it; we simply decided to put it before them. We wanted to make sure that our successes got noticed!

4.4.8 STAY FLEXIBLE AND OPEN-MINDED

There is more than one way of doing something. If the first way does not work, try something else. If you are out of ideas, try asking a colleague. Send your question to a Listserv for information literacy issues, or one for institutions of the same kind as your own. Go back to your research strategy list and update yourself on what has happened at other institutions during the past year. Set up another open-space meeting or gather groups of students to attend focus groups.

4.4.9 BE OPEN TO OPPORTUNITIES

Opportunities may not come along in the order you want or expect. If an opportunity arises, however, take it whenever possible even if it means rearranging something or taking on a new task as a pilot or trial program. One year money for technology might be available, while money for staff is not. Take advantage of the opportunity to upgrade your equipment, even if what you really need is another instructor. Grants and gifts do not always arrive when we would most like to have them, but that does not mean you should reject them if they are offered.

4.4.10 SHARE WITH OTHER LIBRARIANS

The more you share with your colleagues, the easier it will be for everyone to move forward. New points of view or new ways of accomplishing a task may fit nicely into your plan. Why reinvent the wheel? Make sharing your trials and successes part of your plan. Write for your local institutional newsletter. Offer to do a poster session or presentation at a local, regional, or national conference. Post your successes (and failures, if you are really brave) on the appropriate Listservs. Write an article for a scholarly journal.

You will want to provide for the care and maintenance of your plan once it is implemented. This will require periodic review of its parts and timelines. We have suggested some mechanisms for review of your plan below.

Instructions: Brainstorm about what kinds of review instruments will work at your institution.

Venue to plan the next objectives:

_____
_____
_____
_____

Revisit and assess the program goals:

_____
_____
_____
_____

Market the plan and the program:

_____
_____
_____
_____

Report your success widely:

_____
_____
_____
_____

Look for new opportunities:

_____
_____
_____
_____

Share your work with others:

_____
_____
_____
_____

Worksheet 4-C. Construct an Ongoing Review

THE INFORMATION LITERACY (IL) COMPREHENSIVE PLANNING TOOLKIT

OVERVIEW OF IL

While practitioners of information literacy know this story by heart, there may be others who do not. Those new to the world of information literacy may find this brief history useful. In addition, we are frequently called on to explain information literacy to people in administration, funding agencies, and others outside this field of endeavor. The explanation of information literacy that follows may provide practitioners with a ready-made document for that purpose.

WHAT IS INFORMATION LITERACY?

The time we live in is known as the information age. This is so because of the remarkable amount of information that has become easily available to the average person. Anyone who has access to the Internet can get information from numerous sources on just about any topic. There are many sources and formats for information above and beyond the tools that have been available for the past 500 years or so. We are in fact bombarded with information from television, radio, movies, billboards, magazines, newspapers, bulletin boards, Internet, chat rooms, blogs, and government reports.

A quick Internet search on a general subject will demonstrate this fact admirably. How can anyone find and select the specific piece of information wanted when faced with millions of Web sites, newspaper articles, government documents, and personal Web pages on the topic? Having too much information is almost as bad as having no information at all. For those seeking answers to questions that may affect the way they live their lives or how they make important decisions on unknown topics, having too much information results in anxiety. People get stuck and fearful. In addition, the quality of information available is very uneven, ranging from personal opinion to scholarly research. How can people find answers they can trust? How can they select the right information from among the large number of choices they have?

This feeling of confusion and sense of being overwhelmed by the sheer amount of information was identified as early as 1970 by Alvin Toffler in his book *Future Shock*. Toffler coined the term "information overload." He wrote, "In short the more rapidly changing and novel the environment, the more information the individual needs to process in order to make effective, rational decisions. Yet just as there are limits on how much sensory input we can accept, there are built-in constraints on our ability to process information" (Toffler 1970, 351). "While some human responses to novelty are involuntary, others are preceded by conscious thought, and this depends upon our ability to absorb, manipulate, evaluate and retain information" (p. 350).

In the information age, it is essential to effectively receive and respond to information of all kinds in our daily lives. The concept of information overload describes the ever-increasing inability of people to sort, quantify, qualify, use, and discard information. This loss contributes to society's disengagement with critical thinking, intellectual curiosity, and to some degree, our creativity as humans.

Just how significant this problem is today is readily apparent from a brief look at some of the numbers behind the "information explosion." It is claimed that more information has been produced in the past thirty years than in the previous 5,000 years. In 1989, Richard Wurman estimated that a weekday edition of the *New York Times* contains more information than the average person in seventeenth century England was likely to come across in a lifetime (Wurman 1990, 32–35).

The latest "How Much Information" study from the School of Information Management and Systems at the University of California at Berkeley reveals that the amount of information is continuing to grow at an unprecedented rate. In the year 2002 alone, the amount of new information produced would fill 37,000 libraries the size of the Library of Congress (Lyman 2003).

Close to one million new books are published internationally each year—more than 140,000 in the United States alone. These combine with a total published worldwide output of more than 25,000 newspapers, 80,000 magazines and trade periodicals, and 38,000 scholarly journals. Yet, even taking into account the 10.75 billion unique pages of office documents produced each year, the amount of new print-format information is just a drop in the bucket, making up less than 1 percent of all new information produced (Lyman 2003).

The real growth comes from the explosion of new electronic information that is created and stored on hard disks, video- and audiotapes, and other storage media, which is accumulating at rates double to that of only a few years ago (Lyman 2003). In fact, it is estimated that it takes only sixty minutes for the total amount of stored electronic information to double (Mangan 2000). This is in comparison to the approximately five years it takes for all printed information to double (Jungwirth 2002).

Given these numbers, it is easy to understand why many of us feel overwhelmed. Even without searching for information, we are bombarded by advertisements, television and radio broadcasts, phone calls, and e-mail messages. When we surf the Web, we are exploring a universe containing somewhere between 32 and 42 million sites (Lyman 2003).

We are surrounded by information. We have more information than we can possibly process on any topic imaginable. What people find difficult is sorting through the mountain of information they can access to find the specific answers they need, in an appropriate form and at an appropriate intellectual level. Many people have no idea how to go about getting the specific information they need from the mountain of data available to them. Today's information seekers must be instructed in the concepts and skills that will guide them to the accurate, reliable, and appropriate information they want.

This is where information literacy comes in. Information literacy is, then, the ability to ask a question or identify an information need, find appropriate information tools, access information using those tools, evaluate the information obtained for quality and appropriate fit, and answer the question using the information. It is a process vital to life in the twenty-first century. Information literacy can provide us with essential "information survival skills" so that we do not drown in this flood of information.

WHY CREATE A COMPREHENSIVE PLAN FOR INFORMATION LITERACY?

The existence of a comprehensive plan for information literacy at an institution of higher education is a good indication that that institution has made a commitment to information literacy. An information literacy plan shows that the needs of the students, faculty, and staff have been considered. It shows how the information literacy needs of those groups will be met. It is a document in which a vision of the future can be projected. An information literacy plan can be presented to many different audiences: directors, university presidents, boards of governors, alumni, prospective students and their parents, and so on. Even though what is in the plan may not yet be a reality, it will be a road map showing the route, terrain, stages, and destination for the program. It will assist in keeping individuals and groups on track. An information literacy plan can be used for resource allocation in incremental stages, as the plan becomes reality.

Writing a plan for information literacy at an institution of higher education seems like a daunting task. But, when that large task is broken down into small steps and component parts, and each of those parts is addressed individually, the job loses its overwhelming "massiveness," and becomes doable. An entire plan can be assembled for the smaller steps, almost by accretion.

Planning will help identify important aspects of information literacy at a specific institution of higher education. It will delineate who will benefit, how they will benefit, how the outcomes can be measured, and how librarians fit into the delivery of the plan. It will identify resources already available as well as those that will be needed. A plan can also serve as a springboard for future planning.

At the University of Rhode Island, a small group of librarians worked for eighteen months to make our plan for information literacy a reality. The plan can now be found on the library's Web site at www.uri.edu/library/instruction_services/infolitplan.html. We go back to the plan again and again to evaluate what we have done so far, to refresh and renew our vision of where we want to go, to revise our timetables, and to begin new stages of the plan. We also refer others to our plan on a regular basis. The university president recently asked for departments and colleges to send him reports regarding the innovative and exciting programs that are under way at the university. Our plan played a major part in our report. The commissioner of higher education for the state of Rhode Island recently made the same kind of request. Again, our plan played a large role in the report we created.

We have recently been exploring the next step in our plan, and have been delighted to find that our needs assessment and our plan for filling it, parallels the timing of the requests we have been receiving from faculty and students. Because we have a plan in place it is easy to see that (1) we were on the right track when we thought out the plan and (2) we were accurate in our assessment of how long it would take to begin to work on this new stage in our information literacy journey.

Creating an information literacy plan is a multistep process. Breaking the planning process into small steps allows attention to detail, time for thought, and decreased stress for the planners. Tackle your plan one step at a time and give each step all the time and attention it needs. It will add up to a thoughtful and complete plan for information literacy.

How do you know you need an information literacy plan? Presumably, since you are reading this book, you have already ascertained that a plan for the delivery of information literacy concepts and skills is needed. Once you have shown a need for a program of information literacy on your campus, a plan to provide that program becomes a necessity.

SOURCES

Jungwirth, Bernhard, and Bertram C. Bruce. 2002. "Information Overload: Threat or Opportunity." *Reading Online* (February).

Kranich, Nancy. 2000. "Building Information-Smart Communities." *American Libraries* 31, no. 11 (December): 7.

Lyman, Peter, and Hal R. Varian. 2003. "How Much Information," http://www.sims.berkeley.edu/how-much-info-2003 (accessed December 12, 2004).

Mangan, Katherine S. 2000. "In Revamped Library Schools, Information Trumps Books." *Chronicle of Higher Education* 46, no. 31 (April 7): A43–44.

Toffler, Alvin. 1970. *Future Shock.* New York: Bantam.

Wurman, Richard Saul. 1990. *Information Anxiety: What to Do When Information Doesn't Tell You What You Need to Know.* New York: Bantam.

TOOL 2 NEEDS ASSESSMENT BIBLIOGRAPHY

This bibliography contains a sampling of current books and articles about needs assessment. This list will provide the user with a reasonably broad look at theory and practice. Those looking for background information, how-to manuals, or new ideas for needs assessment may find the list useful as a starting point. Needless to say, this list only scratches the surface of the available literature.

Adams, Mignon S., and J. A. Beck. 1995. *User Surveys in College Libraries*. Chicago: College Library Information Packet Committee, College Libraries Section, Association of College and Research Libraries, American Library Association.

Altschuld, James W., and Belle Ruth Witkin. 2000. *From Needs Assessment to Action: Transforming Needs into Solution Strategies*. Thousand Oaks, CA: Sage.

Bourque, Linda B., and Eve P. Fielder. 1995. *How to Conduct Self-Administered and Mail Surveys*. The Survey Kit 3. Thousand Oaks, CA: Sage.

Fink, Arlene. 1995. *How to Ask Survey Questions*. The Survey Kit 2. Thousand Oaks, CA: Sage.

———. 1995. *How to Report on Surveys*. The Survey Kit 9. Thousand Oaks, CA: Sage.

———. 1995. *How to Sample in Surveys*. The Survey Kit 6. Thousand Oaks, CA: Sage.

Fink, Arlene, and Jacqueline Kosecoff. 1998. *How to Conduct Surveys: A Step-by-Step Guide*. 2nd ed. Thousand Oaks, CA: Sage.

Frey, James H., and Sabine Mertens Oishi. 1995. *How to Conduct Interviews by Telephone and in Person*. The Survey Kit 4. Thousand Oaks, CA: Sage.

Grassian, Esther S., and Joan R. Kaplowitz. 2001. *Information Literacy Instruction: Theory and Practice*. New York: Neal-Schuman.

Gupta, Kavita. 1999. *A Practical Guide to Needs Assessment*. San Francisco, CA: Jossey-Bass.

Krueger, Richard A. 1998. *Analyzing and Reporting Focus Group Results*. Focus Group Kit 6. Thousand Oaks, CA: Sage.

———. 1998. *Developing Questions for Focus Groups*. Focus Group Kit 3. Thousand Oaks, CA: Sage.

————. 1998. *Moderating Focus Groups*. Focus Group Kit 4. Thousand Oaks, CA: Sage.

Krueger, Richard A., and Mary Anne Casey. 2000. *Focus Groups: A Practical Guide for Applied Research*. 3rd ed. Thousand Oaks, CA: Sage.

Litwin, Mark. 1995. *How to Measure Survey Reliability and Validity*. The Survey Kit 7. Thousand Oaks, CA: Sage.

Morgan, David L. 1997. *Focus Groups as Qualitative Research*. 2nd ed. Thousand Oaks, CA: Sage.

Morgan, David L., and Alice U. Scannell. 1998. *Planning Focus Groups*. Focus Group Kit 2. Thousand Oaks, CA: Sage.

Queeney, Donna S. 1995. *Assessing Needs in Continuing Education: An Essential Tool for Quality Improvement*. San Francisco, CA: Jossey-Bass.

Westbrook, Lynn. 2001. *Identifying and Analyzing User Needs: A Complete Handbook and Ready-to-Use Assessment Workbook with Disk*. New York: Neal-Schuman.

Witkin, Belle Ruth, and James W. Altschuld. 1995. *Planning and Conducting Needs Assessments: A Practical Guide*. Thousand Oaks, CA: Sage.

PEER INSTITUTIONS BIBLIOGRAPHY

When considering new programs or evaluating existing programs in educational institutions, it is common to compare your own institution to others that are like yours. The sources of statistical data in this list will provide you with numbers you may need for comparative purposes. The sources of methodology will help you select a strategy for comparing your institution with others.

STATISTICAL DATA

The National Center for Educational Statistics (NCES), part of the U.S. Department of Education, gathers data biennially from academic libraries and irregularly from public libraries and school libraries, and state libraries. Through their Web site, reports can be created comparing one library to others. By selecting variables such as geographic location, budget, collection size, or population served, it is possible to generate a list of similar libraries and print or download to spreadsheet a report containing selected data elements.

National Center for Educational Statistics. 2005. *Library Statistics Program: Academic Libraries*. Washington, DC: U.S. Department of Education. Available: http://nces.ed.gov/surveys/libraries/ academic.asp (accessed: July 18, 2005).

National Center for Educational Statistics. 2005. *Library Statistics Program: Public Libraries*. Washington, DC: U.S. Deptartment of Education. Available: http://nces.ed.gov/surveys/libraries/Public .asp (accessed: July 18, 2005).

National Center for Educational Statistics. 2005. *Library Statistics Program: School Libraries*. Washington, DC: U.S. Department of Education. Available: http://nces.ed.gov/surveys/libraries/school .asp (accessed: July 18, 2005).

Besides the data tool for comparing libraries, the NCES Web site provides links to specific publications with data on each type of library. These publications are in PDF format and may be downloaded or viewed online.

National Center for Educational Statistics. 2005. *Library Statistics Program: Publications*. Washington, DC: U.S. Department of Education. Available: http://nces.ed.gov/surveys/libraries/Publications.asp (accessed: July 18, 2005).

Finally, the NCES site also allows the downloading of the raw data files from their surveys.

National Center for Educational Statistics. 2005. *Library Statistics Program: Data Files*. Washington, DC: U.S. Department of Education. Available: http://nces.ed.gov/surveys/libraries/DataFiles.asp (accessed: July 18, 2005).

In addition to the NCES data, academic librarians have a number of other options for gathering statistics to determine peer institutions.

The Association of College and Research Libraries (ACRL) collects statistics on academic libraries by Carnegie classification and publishes them annually in three volumes. Data are available on library collections, expenditures, personnel and public services, Ph.D., faculty, and enrollment statistics, and on selected trends, which have recently included information literacy, library-faculty collaboration, and assessment activities. Volumes may be purchased individually or as a three-volume set. Online access is also available. The latest edition published was in 2004, which provides statistics for the year 2003.

Association of College and Research Libraries. 1998– . *Academic Library Trends and Statistics for Carnegie Classification. Associate of Arts Colleges*. Chicago: Association of College and Research Libraries, annual.

Association of College and Research Libraries. 2000– . *Academic Library Trends and Statistics for Carnegie Classification. Doctoral-Granting Institutions*. Chicago: Association of College and Research Libraries, annual.

Association of College and Research Libraries. 2000– . *Academic Library Trends and Statistics for Carnegie Classification. Master's Colleges and Universities, Baccalaureate Colleges*. Chicago: Association of College and Research Libraries, annual.

If historical data are needed, ACRL's previous statistical surveys were published biennially as:

Association of College and Research Libraries. 1979–1997. *ACRL University Library Statistics*. Chicago: Association of College and Research Libraries, biennial.

For those on a tight budget or a deadline, summary information from ACRL's statistical surveys is freely available on the ACRL Web site. Data from the 1998 to the current 2003 survey are available.

Association of College and Research Libraries. 1998–2003. "Statistical Summaries for Academic Libraries." Summary reports from

ACRL's *Academic Library Trends and Statistics.* Chicago: Association of College and Research Libraries. Available: www.ala.org/ala/acrl/acrlpubs/acadlibrarystats/academiclibrary .htm.

Larger academic libraries may wish to compare themselves with libraries in the Association of Research Libraries (ARL), an organization of the top 123 research libraries in North America, both academic and public, in terms of resources. Current ARL statistics include quantitative and qualitative data on collections, staffing, expenditures, library services, and library and university characteristics, and are freely available online. Through an interactive interface, users can construct data queries and select the body of data they would like to search. It is possible to generate rankings of ARL institutions, create summary statistics for a selection of libraries, retrieve data for specific libraries, generate charts and graphs, and to download data to spreadsheet format. In addition to the interactive format, an electronic .pdf version of recent years of *ARL Statistics* may be downloaded from the ARL Web site. Compilations of selected ARL statistical data are also available in print format from the organization.

Association of Research Libraries. 1962–2003. *ARL Statistics.* Interactive edition. Washington, DC: Association of Research Libraries, annual. Available: http://fisher.lib.virginia.edu/arl/index.html.

Association of Research Libraries. 1962–2004. *ARL Statistics.* Washington, DC: Association of Research Libraries, annual. Years 1999 through 2004 available online at: http://www.arl.org /stats/arlstat/index.html.

Finally, academic librarians who are not certain of the Carnegie classification of their institution may consult the Carnegie Foundation's Web site for a description of the categories, listings of institutions by category, and an index of institutions with the category of each given.

The Carnegie Foundation for the Advancement of Teaching. 2000. *The Carnegie Classification of Institutions of Higher Education.* Menlo Park, CA: The Carnegie Foundation for the Advancement of Teaching. Available: www.carnegiefoundation.org /Classification/index.htm.

METHODOLOGY

Following is a short bibliography of selected sources addressing methodologies of conducting peer-institution comparisons.

Anderl, Robert G. 1996. "Your Peer Groups and You: How Do You Stack Up?" *PNLA Quarterly* 60 (Winter): 20–25.

Arnold, Carolyn L. 1997. "Using National Data Sets to Create Comparable National Statistics for the Student Characteristics and

Outcomes in Community Colleges." Hayward, CA: Chabot College. Available as ERIC Document ED421197.

Brinkman, Paul T. 1987. "Effective Interinstitutional Comparisons." In *Conducting Interinstitutional Comparisons,* edited by Paul T. Brinkman, 103–108. New Directions for Institutional Research, no. 53. San Francisco, CA: Jossey-Bass.

Brinkman, Paul, and Jack Krakower. 1983. *Comparative Data for Administrators in Higher Education.* Boulder, CO: National Center for Higher Education Management Systems (NCHEMS).

Brinkman, Paul T., and Deborah J. Teeter. 1987. "Methods for Selecting Comparison Groups." In *Conducting Interinstitutional Comparisons,* edited by Paul T. Brinkman, 5–23. New Directions for Institutional Research, no. 53. San Francisco, CA: Jossey-Bass.

Christal, Melodie E., and John R. Wittstruck. 1987. "Sources of Comparative Data." In *Conducting Interinstitutional Comparisons,* edited by Paul T. Brinkman, 25–47. New Directions for Institutional Research, no. 53. San Francisco, CA: Jossey-Bass.

Cleaver, G. S. 1981. "Analysis to Determine a Ranking in Similarity for Institutions in Higher Education." Paper presented at the Annual Conference of the Society for College and University Planning, Omaha, Nebraska, July 12–15, 1981. Lawrence, KS: Office of Institutional Research and Planning, University of Kansas.

Dunn, John A., Jr. 1987. "Setting Up a Data-Sharing Project." In *Conducting Interinstitutional Comparisons,* edited by Paul T. Brinkman, 49–57. New Directions for Institutional Research, no. 53. San Francisco, CA: Jossey-Bass.

Elsass, J. E., and P. E. Lingenfelter. 1980. *An Identification of College and University Peer Groups.* Springfield, IL: Illinois Board of Education.

Hurley, Rodney G. 2002. "Identification and Assessment of Community College Peer Institution Selection Systems." *Community College Review* 29, no. 4 (Spring): 1–27.

Korb, Roslyn. 1982. "Clusters of Colleges and Universities: An Empirically Determined System." Washington, DC: National Center for Educational Statistics. Available as ERIC Document ED227797.

Lang, Daniel W. "Similarities and Differences: Measuring Diversity and Selecting Peers in Higher Education." 2000. *Higher Education* 39, no. 1 (January): 93–129.

McCoy, Marilyn. 1987. "Interinstitutional Analysis at the System and State Level." In *Conducting Interinstitutional Comparisons,* edited by Paul T. Brinkman, 73–81. New Directions for Institutional Research, no. 53. San Francisco, CA: Jossey-Bass.

Peterson, M. W., ed. 1976. *Benefiting from Interinstitutional Research.* New Directions for Institutional Research, no. 12. San Francisco, CA: Jossey-Bass.

Rawson, Thomas M., D. P. Hoyt, and Deborah J. Teeter. 1983. "Identifying 'Comparable' Institutions." *Research in Higher Education* 18, no. 3: 299–310.

Russell, Alene Bycer, and Susan Winter. 2002. *Compendium of National Data Sources on Higher Education.* Denver, CO: State Higher Education Executive Officers, SHEEO Online Access to Resources (SOAR). Available: www.sheeo.org/soar/compendium .asp?compid=2. Last updated, April 23, 2002.

Smart, J. C., C. F. Elton, and R. O. Martin. 1980. "Qualitative and Conventional Indices of Benchmark Institutions." In *Meeting the Challenges of the Eighties: Redirection of Resources for Renewal: Twentieth Annual Forum, April 27–May 1, 1980. Peachtree Plaza Hotel, Atlanta, Georgia,* by Association for Institutional Research. Tallahassee, FL: Association for Institutional Research.

Teeter, Deborah J. 1983. "The Politics of Comparing Data with Other Institutions." In *The Politics and Pragmatics of Institutional Research,* edited by J. W. Firnberg and W. F. Lasher, 39–48. New Directions for Institutional Research, no. 38. San Francisco, CA: Jossey-Bass.

Teeter, Deborah J., and Melodie E. Christal. 1986/87. "Establishing Peer Groups: A Comparison of Methodologies." *Planning for Higher Education* 15, no. 2 (Spring): 8–17.

Terenzini, P. T., L. Hartmark, W. G. Lorang, Jr., and R. C. Shirley. 1980. "A Conceptual and Methodological Approach to the Identification of Peer Institutions." *Research in Higher Education* 12, no. 4: 347–364.

Weeks, Susan F., Dave Puckett, and Ruth Daron. 2000. "Developing Peer Groups for the Oregon University System: From Politics to Analysis (and Back)." *Research in Higher Education* 14, no. 1 (February): 1–20.

Whiteley, Meredith A., and Frances K. Stage. 1987. "Institutional Uses of Comparative Data." In *Conducting Interinstitutional Comparisons,* edited by Paul T. Brinkman, 59–71. New Directions for Institutional Research, no. 53. San Francisco, CA: Jossey-Bass.

Zhao, Jisehn, and Donald C. Dean. 1997. "Selecting Peer Institutions: A Hybrid Approach." Paper presented at the thirty-seventh annual forum of the Association for Institutional Research, Orlando, FL, May 18–21, 1997. New York: The College of St. Rose. Available as ERIC Document ED410877.

TOOL 4

SOURCES FOR IL DEFINITIONS

As you are thinking about what to call the information literacy (IL) program you create and how to define it, you may want to know something about how this process was undertaken in other places. The sources in this list will provide you with ideas that can be applied to your local culture.

American Association of School Librarians
www.ala.org/aaslTemplate.cfm?Section=aaslinfolit

American Library Association—ALA
Presidential Committee on Information Literacy: Final Report. January 10, 1989.
www.ala.org/ala/acrl/acrlpubs/whitepapers/presidential.htm

Association of College and Research Libraries—ACRL
Institute for Information Literacy Executive Board. Chicago: American Library Association, 2003.
www.ala.org/ala/acrl/acrlissues/acrlinfolit/infolitoverview/introtoinfolit/int
    roinfolit.htm
Callison, Daniel. 2003. "Key Words in Instruction: Information Fluency."
    School Library Media Activities Monthly 20, no. 4 (December):
    38–39.

Definitions of Information Literacy and Related Terms from the University of South Florida, August 2003
http://bulldogs.tlu.edu/mdibbledoril/definitions.html
Grassian, Esther S., and Joan R. Kaplowitz. 2001. *Information Literacy
    Instruction: Theory and Practice.* New York: Neal-Schuman.

Directory of Online Resources for Information Literacy (DORIL)
http://bulldogs.tlu.edu/mdibble/doril/

National Forum for Information Literacy
www.infolit.org/definitions/index.html
Shapiro, Jeremy J., and Shelley K. Hughes. 1996. "Information
    Literacy as a Liberal Art." *Educom Review* 3, no. 2 (March/April):
    31–35. Available: http://www.educause.edu/pub/er/review
    /reviewarticles/31231.html

TOOL 5 ASSOCIATIONS SUPPORTING IL

The Web sites on this list belong to organizations that support programs of information literacy by providing information, links, best practices, contacts, examples, and advice.

ACRL Information Literacy Initiatives
www.ala.org/ala/acrl/acrlissues/acrlinfolit/informationliteracy.htm

ALA Library Instruction Round Table (LIRT)
www3.baylor.edu/LIRT/

American Association of School Librarians
www.ala.org/ala/aasl/aaslissues/aaslinfolit/informationliteracy1.htm

American Library Association (ALA)
www.ala.org

Association of College and Research Libraries (ACRL) Instruction Section
www.ala.org/ala/acrl/aboutacrl/acrlsections/instruction/homepage.htm

LOEX Clearinghouse for Library Instruction
www.emich.edu/public/loex/loex.html

National Forum on Information Literacy
www.infolit.org/

STANDARDS AND GUIDELINES FOR IL

These documents list the standards and best practices for addressing those standards at various educational levels. Each part of your plan should be linked to one or more of the appropriate standards.

Characteristics of Programs of Information Literacy that Illustrate Best Practices: A Guideline—Best Practices Initiative, Institute for Information Literacy
www.ala.org/ala/acrl/acrlstandards/characteristics.htm

Information Literacy Competency Standards for Higher Education
www.ala.org/ala/acrl/acrlstandards/informationliteracycompetency.htm

Objectives for Information Literacy Instruction: A Model Statement for Academic Librarians
www.ala.org/ala/acrl/acrlstandards/objectivesinformation.htm

Resources for School Library Media Program Support—Standards and Guidelines
www.ala.org/aaslTemplate.cfm?Section=resourceguides&Template=
    /ContentManagement/ContentDisplay.cfm&ContentID=15419

TOOL **7**

MARKETING BIBLIOGRAPHY

As part of your planning process you should include specific plans for how to market the separate parts of your plan to your constituencies. The following bibliography provides a small sampling of the marketing literature specific to libraries and library programs.

Akers, Cynthia, Nanette P. Martin, and Terri P. Summey. 2000. "Teaching the Teachers: Library Instruction through Professional Development Courses." *Research Strategies* 17, no. 2/3: 215–221.

American Library Association. 2005. "School Library Campaign." www.ala.org/ala/pio/campaign/schoollibrary/schoollibrary.htm (accessed June 10, 2005).

American Library Association. 2004. "ACRL's Marketing @ Your Library Page." www.ala.org/marketing (accessed June 10, 2005).

Beck, Susan E., and Kate Manuel. 2003. "Folding Information Literacy into the General Education Mix: Recipes for Getting Started." In Integrating Information Literacy into the College Experience, edited by Julia K. Nims, Randal Baier, and Eric Bullard, 11–17. Papers presented at the thirtieth national LOEX Library Instruction Conference, Ypsilanti, Michigan, May 10–11, 2002. Ann Arbor, MI: Pierian Press.

Blauer, Ann T. 1995. "Librarian, Clone Thyself! Using a Video to Promote Your Library Service." In The Seventh Off-Campus Library Services Conference Proceedings, compiled by Carol J. Jacob, 17–23. San Diego, California, October 25–27. Mount Pleasant, MI: Central Michigan University.

Cheuk, Wai-yi B. 1999. "A Marketing Approach to the Design of Education Programs for Undergraduates." *Reference Services Review* 27, no. 1 (January): 62–68.

Davidson, Jeanne R. 2001. "Faculty and Student Attitudes toward Credit Courses for Library Skills." *College and Research Libraries* 62, no. 2 (March): 155–163.

Fosmire, Michael. 2001. "Bibliographic Instruction in Physics Libraries: A Survey of Current Practice and Tips for Marketing BI." *Science and Technology Libraries* 19, no. 2 (Winter): 25–34.

Furlong, Katherine, and Andrew B. Crawford. 1999. "Marketing Your Services through Your Students." *Computers in Libraries* 19, no. 8 (September): 22–24+.

Kachel, Debra E. 2003. "Partners for Success: A School Library Advocacy Training Program for Principals." *Knowledge Quest* 32, no. 2 (November/December): 17–19.

Kirkendall, Carolyn A., ed. 1986. "Marketing Instructional Services: Applying Private Sector Techniques to Plan and Promote Bibliographic Instruction." Papers presented at the thirteenth Library Instruction Conference, Eastern Michigan University, May 3–4, 1984. Ann Arbor, MI: Pierian Press.

Lawson, Mollie D. 2000. "Reaching the Masses: Marketing a Library Instruction Course to Incoming Freshmen." *Research Strategies* 17, no. 1 (Spring): 45–49.

Lehman, Kathy. 2000. "Promoting Library Advocacy and Information Literacy from an 'Invisible Library.'" *Teacher Librarian* 29, no. 4 (April): 27–30.

Neely, Teresa Y., Naomi Lederer, and Awilda Reyes. 2001. "Instruction and Outreach at Colorado State University Libraries." *The Reference Librarian* no. 67–68 (February): 273–287.

Nims, Julia K. 1999. "Marketing Library Instruction Services: Changes and Trends." *Reference Services Review* 27, no. 3: 249–253.

Price, Ward. 2001. "If You Build It, Will They Come? How Do We Encourage Students (and Faculty) to Come to the Library for Instruction?" In Library User Education in the New Millennium: Blending Tradition, Trends, and Innovation, edited by Julia K. Nims and Ann Andrew, 161–162. Papers presented at the twenty-seventh national LOEX Library Instruction Conference, Houston, Texas, March 11–13, 1999. Ann Arbor, MI: Pierian Press.

Rhodes, Naomi J., and Judith M. Davis. 2001. "Using Service Learning to Get Positive Reactions in the Library." *Computers in Libraries* 21, no. 1 (January): 32–35.

Rockwell-Kincanon, Janeanne. 2001. "Got Library? Musings on Marketing Information Literacy." *OLA Quarterly* 7, no. 2 (Summer): 16–17.

Schwartz, Diane G. 1984. "Bibliographic Instruction: A Public Relations Perspective." *Medical Reference Services Quarterly* 3 (Summer): 43–49.

Swaine, Cynthia W. 2001. "Developing, Marketing, and Evaluating Web-based Library and Information Skills Tutorials." *Virginia Libraries* 47, no. 3 (July/August/September): 5–8.

Warren, Rebecca, Sherman Hayes, and Donna Gunter. 2001. "Segmentation Techniques for Expanding a Library Instruction Market: Evaluating and Brainstorming." *Research Strategies* 18, no. 3: 171–180.

Weaver, Patricia. 1997. Marketing Library Instruction to Adults. *College and Research Libraries News* no. 7 (July/August): 493–494.

White, Marjorie V. 2003. "Information Literacy Programs: Successful Paradigms for Stimulating and Promoting Faculty Interest and Involvement." *The Reference Librarian* no. 79/80 (November): 323–334.

TOOL 8

IL IN THE DISCIPLINES—BY THE TEACHING METHODS COMMITTEE OF ACRL

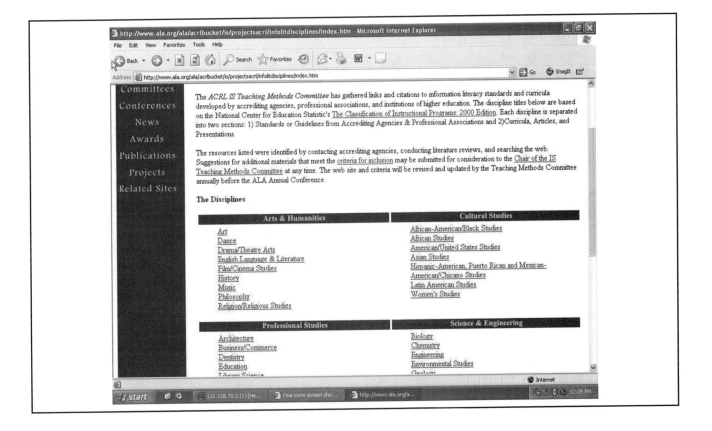

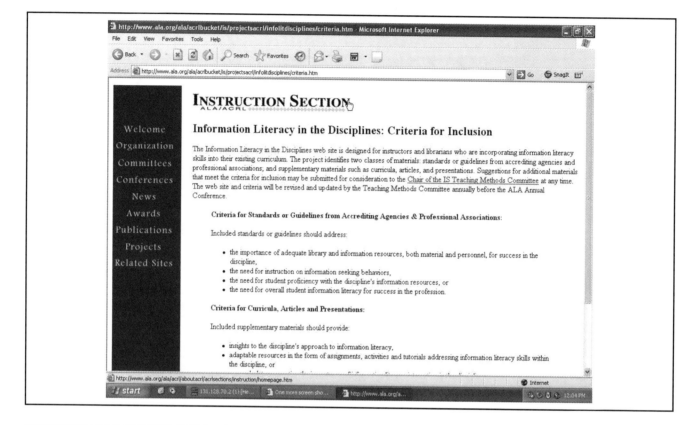

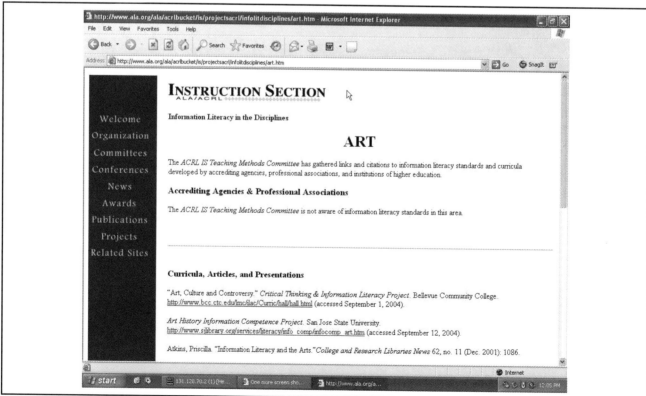

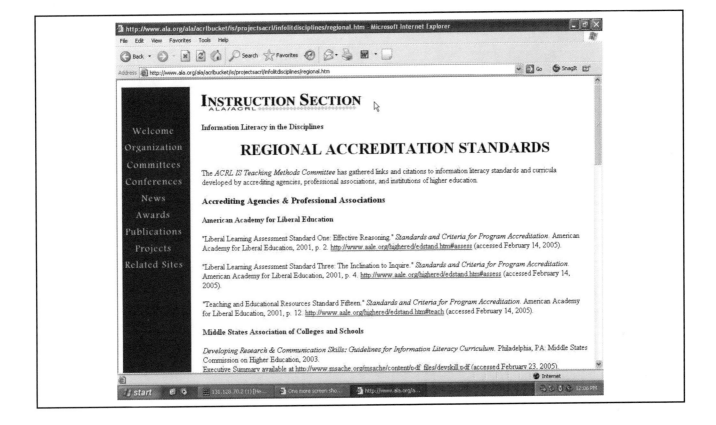

III MODEL REAL WORLD PLANS

K-6 PLAN OF PINE POINT SCHOOL, STONINGTON, CONNECTICUT

This design using a "year of study" at a university can be compared to the same approach used at a grade school. Pine Point School in Stonington, Connecticut, introduces progressively sophisticated skills as the children pass through grades K-6.

Concepts, Skills, and Activities (Kindergarten)

- a. Listening skills (books, storytelling, flannelboard, and video/DVD)
- b. Lending (versus renting or buying)
- c. Book care and responsibility for return
- d. Selection of books
- e. Check-out procedures
- f. Definition of terms: author, illustrator, spine and spine label
- g. Alphabetical arrangement of easy books by first letter of author's last name

Assessment

Students in grades K-3 do not receive any formal written grade or evaluation. In the event of a continued problem with participation or attentiveness, the librarian speaks to the classroom teachers.

Concepts, Skills, and Activities (Grade 1)

NOTE: Concepts marked with an asterisk are review and extension of concepts covered in the previous year(s).

- a. *Listening skills
- b. Recalling, paraphrasing, retelling, and/or dramatizing stories

    c. Telling stories from pictures

    d. Locating books on the easy shelves by author

    e. Recognizing certain authors and illustrators

    f. Basic organization of the Pine Point School Library (Easy, Reference, Fiction, Nonfiction, Audiovisual software, and Biography sections)

    g. Introduction to computerized "card" catalog (location, definition)

    h. Introduction to nonfiction books

    i. *Proper book care etiquette

    j. *Definition of terms: author, illustrator, spine, title, spine label

Concepts, Skills, and Activities (Grade 2)

    a. *Listening skills, retelling, paraphrasing, and dramatizing

    b. Online (computerized) "card" catalog—using it to locate books with help; simple keyword searches; using asterisk ("wildcard") symbol for most effective searching

    c. *Finding and returning easy books to proper place on shelf

    d. Encyclopedia introduction—*New Book of Knowledge*

    e. Fiction versus nonfiction

    f. Strategies for selecting books for leisure reading (especially early chapter books)

    g. *Authors/illustrators and their works—for example, Bill Peet, Chris Van Allsburg, Arnold Lobel

    h. Southern Black folklore

    i. *Definition of terms: author, title, illustrator, spine, spine label

Concepts, Skills, and Activities (Grade 3)

    a. Online (computerized) "card" catalog

       1. *Simple keyword searches to find books for leisure reading

       2. *Using the asterisk ("wildcard") symbol to widen a search

3. Introduction to simple subject headings

4. Call numbers and how books are arranged on shelf in call number order

5. Finding books on the shelf with help

b. Introduction to information found on spine of book

c. *Basic sections of library (fiction, nonfiction, biography, audiovisual software, reference, easy)

d. *Using encyclopedias for reports (*New Book of Knowledge, World Book*; demonstration of *World Book Online Encyclopedia*)

e. Fiction versus nonfiction

f. *Strategies for selecting recreational reading (e.g., favorite author or topic; new book lists; recommendations from friends, parents, teachers; cover and jacket blurb, and so on)

g. Genres—fables, historical fiction

h. Idioms and homonyms (Fred Gwunne books)

i. Definition of terms: characters, setting, plot, dialog, index, table of contents

Concepts, Skills and Activities (Grade 4)

a. Online (computerized) "card" catalog

1. *Simple keyword searches to find books for leisure and research

2. *Using the asterisk ("wildcard") symbol to widen a search

3. *Call numbers—different types

4. Locating all types of materials using call numbers

5. Using subject headings to find nonfiction

b. Location skills—Location relay (detailed floor plan)

c. *Strategies for choosing books for leisure reading

d. *Information found on a book's spine

e. *Encyclopedia—detailed look at types of sources ("pathfinder") to locate information on sea animal of choice (in conjunction with classroom project)

f. Following a suggested list of types of sources ("pathfinder") to locate information on sea animal of choice (in conjunction with classroom project)

    g. Alliteration and alphabetizing (to third letter)

    h. Definition of terms: title page, dedication, preface, appendix, glossary, bibliography, biography, epilog, prolog, copyright date and symbol, Dewey Decimal Classification System

Assessment

Students in Grade 4 do a fair amount of written work. Worksheets are often corrected on the spot or, if time does not allow, corrected and returned to the students in the following class. Work remains in the library in folders until the end of the year. Fourth graders receive comments in December and June discussing their level of participation and effort and the quality of their resulting work.

Concepts, Skills and Activities (Overview)

    I. Library equipment, procedures and etiquette, book care

      a. How to check out a book

      b. Due dates and responsibility for return of materials

      c. Concept of loan versus rental or purchase

      d. Number of items that may be borrowed at one time

      e. Proper care of books and software

      f. Use of computers in library

    II. Language and literature appreciation

      a. Familiarity with specific authors and illustrators

      b. Critical listening and viewing skills

      c. Finding the main idea, paraphrasing, and dramatizing stories

      d. Selecting fiction for recreation as well as book reports

      e. Learning to recognize and appreciate various genres (examples include fairy tales, tall tales, poetry, mystery, science fiction, historical fiction)

      f. Miscellaneous aspects of language as they relate to specific books (e.g., idioms, homonyms, alliteration)

III. Organization of the library

    a. The online ("card") catalog

        1. Information found in a catalog record

        2. Different searching methods—keyword, author, subject, title

        3. Alternative strategies to widen search (too few items found) or refine search (too many items found)

        4. Call numbers

    b. Basic organization of the Pine Point School Library (easy, reference, fiction, nonfiction, audiovisual, and biography sections)

    c. Fiction versus nonfiction

    d. Dewey Decimal Classification System

IV. Using library resources to locate specific information

    a. Identification of parts of a book

    b. Pamphlet file

    c. Biographical sources

    d. Almanacs

    e. Encyclopedias (both general and specialized, print and online)

    f. Magazine indexes (*Children's Magazine Guide; MiddleSearch* [online])

    g. Using periodicals (both hard copy and online)

    h. Online database access and searching (*MiddleSearch*; *iConn)*

    i. Cautions about using Internet sources; how to critically evaluate them

    j. Operation of audiovisual equipment and computers

    k. Miscellaneous reference works

V. Database searching skills

    a. Using Boolean search operators (AND, OR, NOT)

    b. Wildcards and truncation (the "magic star"*)

    c. Keyword versus subject searching

VI. Research and reporting techniques

    a. Selecting materials appropriate to the assignment

    b. Note taking and paraphrasing

    c. Introduction to bibliographies

NOTE: Concepts marked with an asterisk are review and extension of concepts covered in the previous year(s).

Concepts, Skills, and Activities (Grade 5)

    a. Online (computerized) "card" catalog

        1. Searching by author, title, or subject (in addition to keyword)

        2. Meaning of each piece of information found on an online record

        3. *Using the asterisk ("wildcard") symbol to widen a search

        4. Using subject searches to locate fiction books for book reports (limiting a search to a certain material type)

        5. *Locating materials in all parts of the library using call numbers

    b. *Location skills—location relay (detailed floor plan)

    c. Locating a variety of resources for a report (in conjunction with classroom vertebrate project)

    d. Genres and how to locate titles within them (in conjunction with classroom book reports, e.g., historical fiction)

    e. *Children's Magazine Guide*

    f. Almanacs

Assessment

Students do a good deal of written work. Worksheets are often corrected on the spot or, if time does not allow, corrected and returned to the students in the following class. Work remains in the library in folders until the end of the year. Students receive comments in December and June discussing their level of participation and effort and the quality of their resulting work.

Concepts, Skills and Activities (Grade 6)

I. Organization of library

    a. Dewey Decimal Classification System

        1. Understanding decimal nature (in conjunction with math class)

        2. Shelving nonfiction by Dewey number

II. Using library resources to find specific information

    a. Periodicals online (*MiddleSearch*)

    b. Selecting appropriate databases (EBSCOHost Web)

    c. Brief introduction to *iConn* databases

III. Research and reporting techniques

    a. Paraphrasing and note taking

    b. Introduction to bibliographies (works cited)

    c. Location of appropriate materials for bird report

IV. Database searching skills

    a. Introduction to database terms: record, field, database, sorting/indexing

    b. Production and manipulation of class database (indexing/sorting, searching)

    c. Boolean search operators (AND, OR, NOT) production of "human Venn Diagrams"

Assessment

At the end of each term students in grade 6 receive comments assessing the following:

1. Quality of written work
2. Attentiveness and participation in class
3. Ability to work both independently and as a member of a group
4. General attitude

In the spring term, the source cards and bibliographies are graded and the resulting two quiz grades are included in the Science average for that term.

AUSTIN COMMUNITY COLLEGE LIBRARY, AUSTIN, TEXAS

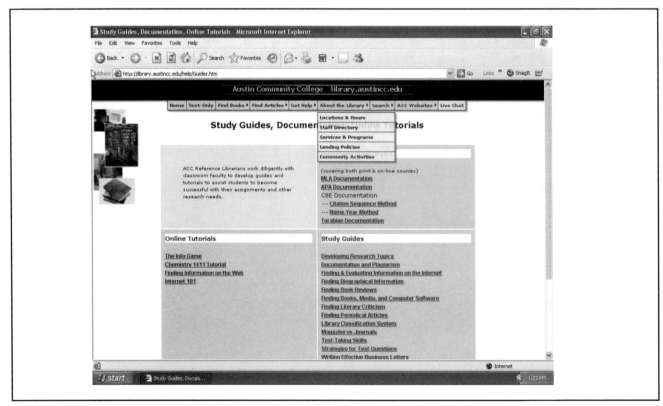

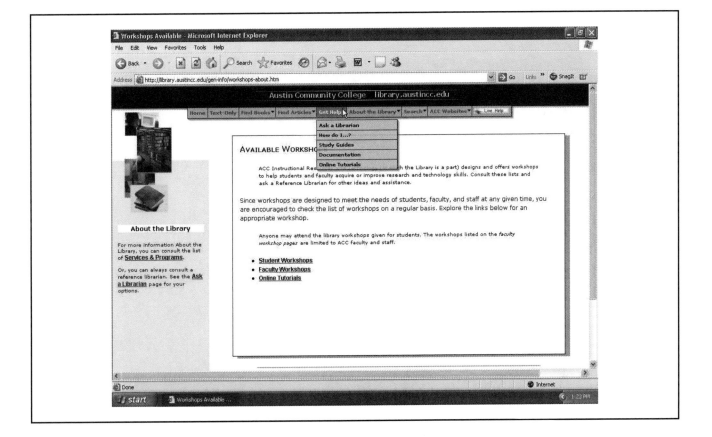

PLAN 3

VOGEL LIBRARY, WARTBURG COLLEGE, WAVERLY, IOWA

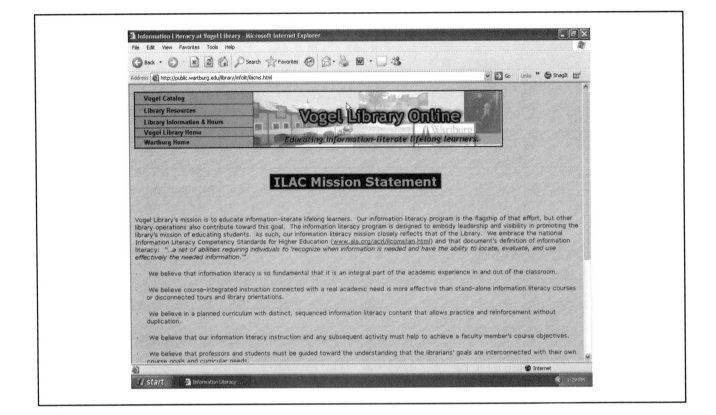

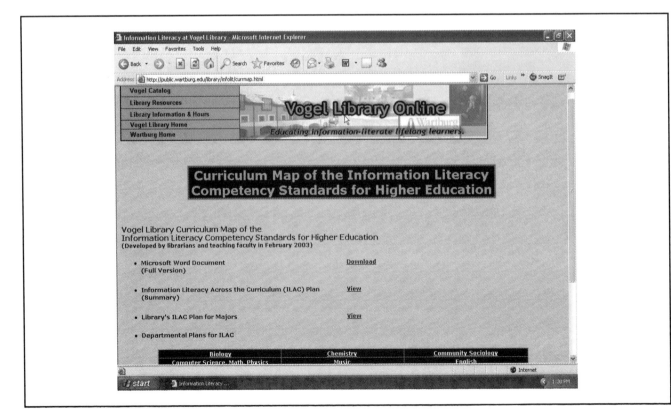

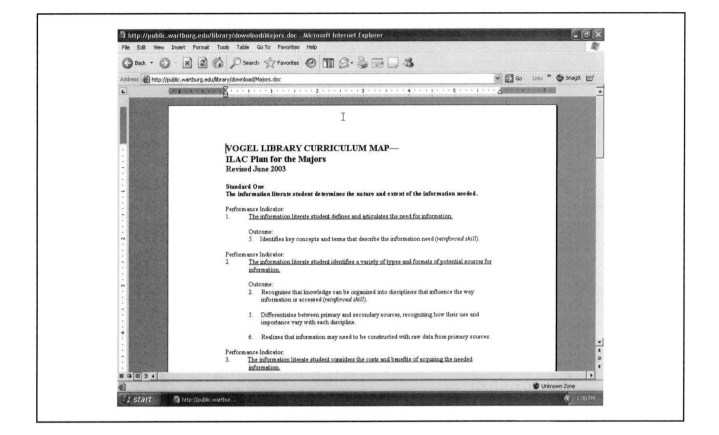

ROGER WILLIAMS UNIVERSITY LIBRARIES, BRISTOL, RHODE ISLAND

PLAN 5

UNIVERSITY OF CALIFORNIA LIBRARIES, LOS ANGELES, CALIFORNIA

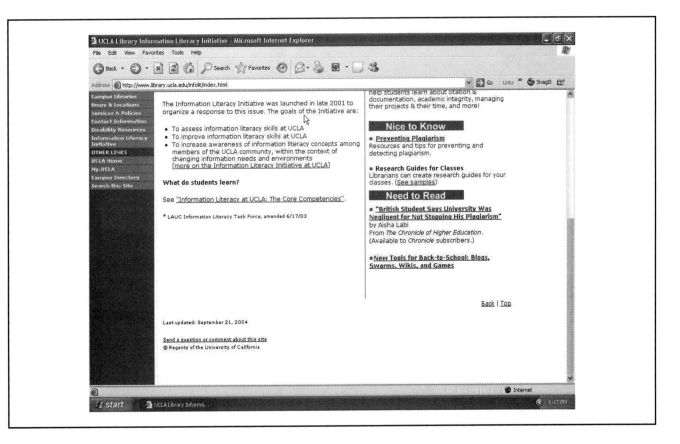

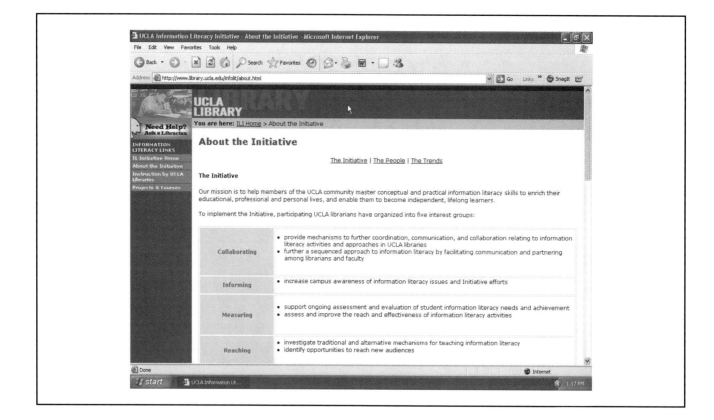

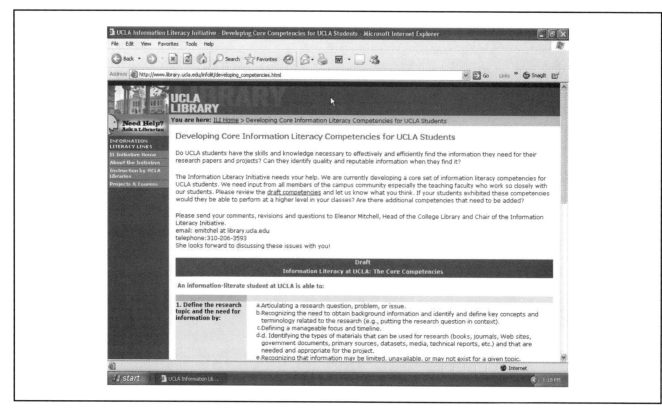

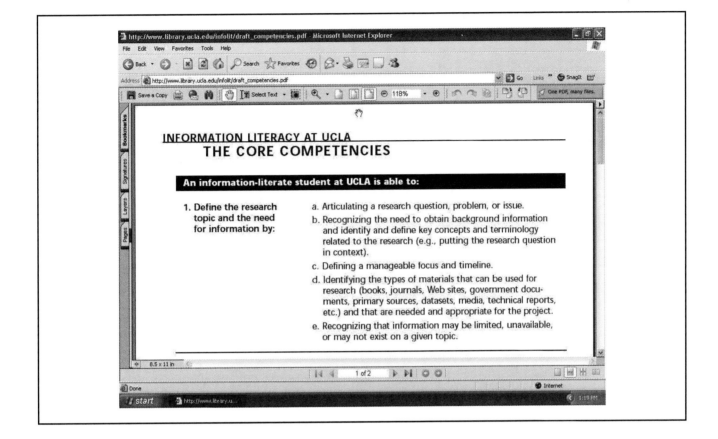

PLAN 6

STEWART LIBRARY, WEBER STATE UNIVERSITY, OGDEN, UTAH

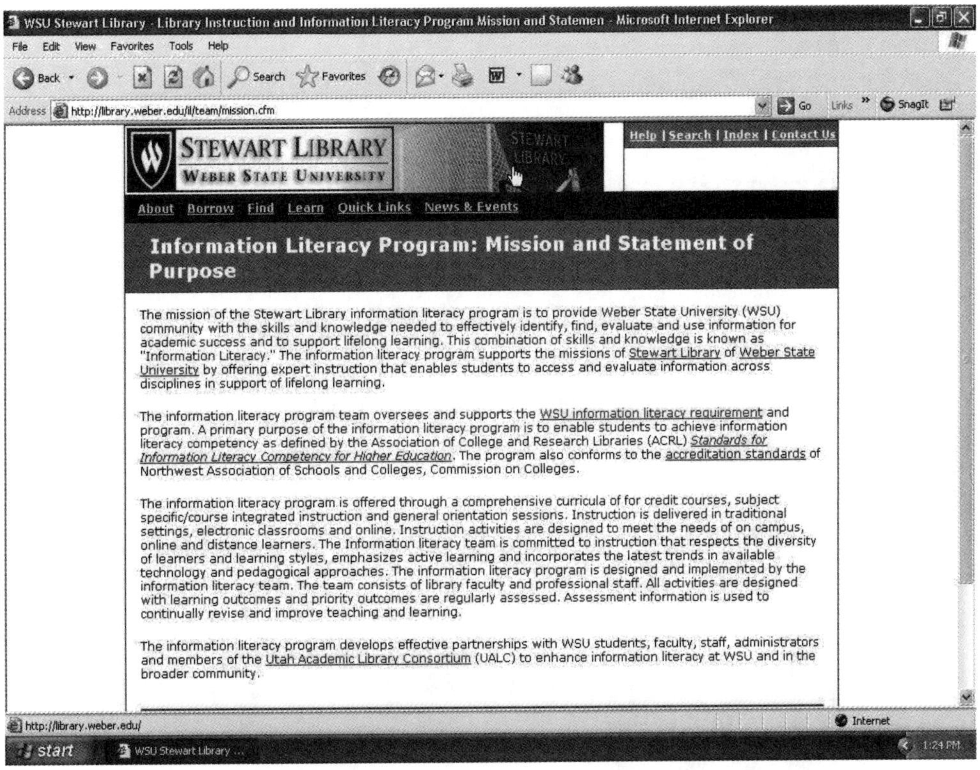

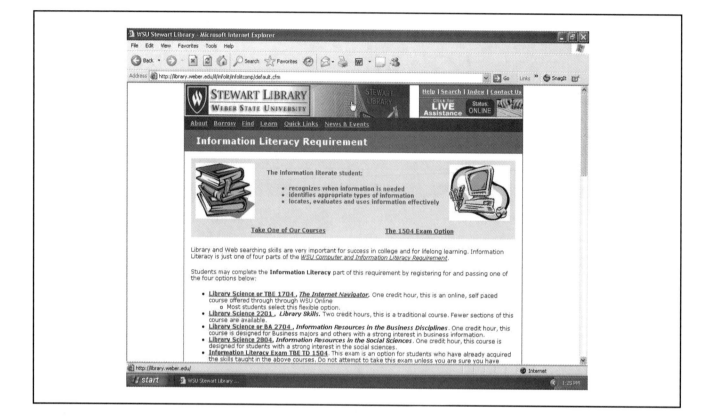

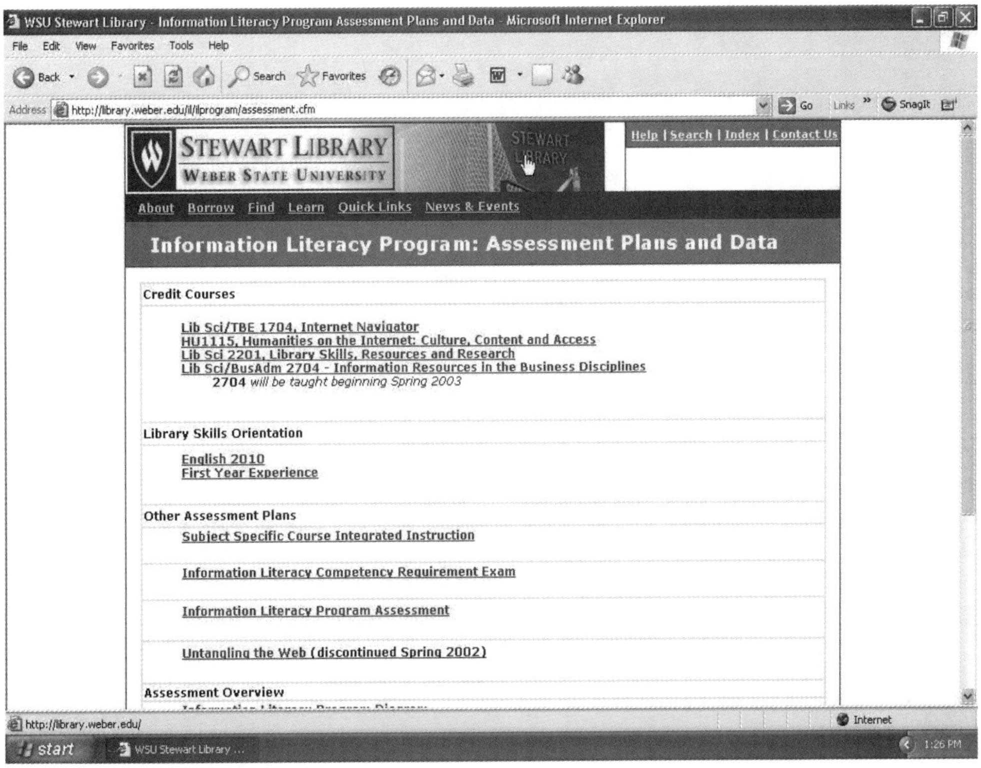
WSU Stewart Library - Information Literacy Program Assessment Plans and Data - Microsoft Internet Explorer
File Edit View Favorites Tools Help
Back
Search
Favorites
Address
http://library.weber.edu/il/ilprogram/assessment.cfm
Go
Links
SnagIt
STEWART LIBRARY
WEBER STATE UNIVERSITY
Help | Search | Index | Contact Us
About Borrow Find Learn Quick Links News & Events
Information Literacy Program: Assessment Plans and Data
Credit Courses
Lib Sci/TBE 1704, Internet Navigator
HU1115, Humanities on the Internet: Culture, Content and Access
Lib Sci 2201, Library Skills, Resources and Research
Lib Sci/BusAdm 2704 - Information Resources in the Business Disciplines
2704 will be taught beginning Spring 2003
Library Skills Orientation
English 2010
First Year Experience
Other Assessment Plans
Subject Specific Course Integrated Instruction
Information Literacy Competency Requirement Exam
Information Literacy Program Assessment
Untangling the Web (discontinued Spring 2002)
Assessment Overview
http://library.weber.edu/
Internet
start
WSU Stewart Library ...
1:26 PM

PLAN 7

HYPERLINKED LIST OF MODEL IL PLANS

UNIVERSITY LIBRARIES

American University
www.library.american.edu/about/services/instruction/forum.html

California State University, Fullerton
http://guides.library.fullerton.edu/infocomp/

California State University, San Marcos
http://library.csusm.edu/departments/ilp/overview.asp

Florida International University Libraries
www.fiu.edu/~library/ili/outcomes.html

Idaho State University
www.isu.edu/departments/acadaff/TOC/fluetech/literacy.html

James Madison University Libraries
www.lib.jmu.edu/instruction

Miami University Libraries' Information Literacy Plan
www.lib.muohio.edu/infolit/info_lit_plan.pdf

Philadelphia University
www.philau.edu/tltr/information_literacy.htm

Roger Williams University
http://library.rwu.edu/about/infolit.html

University of Montevallo
http://olddev.montevallo.edu/library/FacultyInfo/
     InformationLiteracyPlan.shtm

University of Rhode Island
www.uri.edu/library/instruction_services/infolitplan.html

Weber State University
http://library.weber.edu/il/ilprogram/default.cfm

COLLEGE LIBRARIES

Elmhurst College
www.elmhurst.edu/library/infolit

Five Colleges of Ohio
www.denison.edu/collaborations/ohio5/grant/

St. Olaf College
www.stolaf.edu/library/instruction/infolit/action1.html

Wartburg College
www.wartburg.edu/library/infolit/index.html

York College of Pennsylvania
www.ycp.edu/library/ifl/etext/ethome.html

COMMUNITY COLLEGES

Hillsboro Community College
www.hccfl.edu/library/pdfs/InfoLitPolityStatePlan.pdf

Owensboro Community and Technical College
www.octc.kctcs.edu/library/infoliteracy.htm

INDEX

ABOUT THE AUTHORS

Joanna M. Burkhardt is Associate Professor and Head Librarian at the University of Rhode Island Providence Campus Library. She is a member of the University of Rhode Island Libraries Management Team. She is also an active member of the American Library Association, the Association of College and Research Libraries, and the Rhode Island Library Association. Burkhardt has been Chair of the URI Libraries Faculty Development Committee and Chair of the URI Libraries Curriculum Committee. She has represented URI on a number of Rhode Island Higher Education Library Information Network (HELIN) Consortium Committees. She teaches sections of URI's course in information literacy and has recently begun developing a graduate level seminar for students in the Communications Department. She has authored a number of articles on library management, consortium issues, and information literacy. She is coauthor of *Teaching Information Literacy: 35 Practical, Standards-based Exercises for College Students* (Chicago: ALA, 2003), jburkhardt@uri.edu.

Mary C. MacDonald is Associate Professor Librarian in the Reference Unit of the University Library, University of Rhode Island, where, as Information Literacy Librarian, she coordinates the information literacy program and teaches LIB 120: "Introduction to Information Literacy." She is an active member of the Association of College and Research Libraries Instruction Section—ACRL/New England Chapter. She is a member of the University of Rhode Island's University College General Education Committee (UCGE) and of the UCGE Implementation Advisory Group. She was a 2003–2004 Teaching Fellow at the university. She is coauthor of *Teaching Information Literacy: 35 Practical, Standards-based Exercises for College Students* (Chicago: ALA, 2003), marymac@uri.edu.

Andrée J. Rathemacher is Associate Professor in the Technical Services Department of the University Library at the University of Rhode Island where she is the Serials Librarian and business bibliographer. She was actively involved in the Library's information literacy program from its inception. She is an active member of the American Library Association and the Association for College and Research Libraries. She has been Chair of ACRL/New England Chapter's Business Librarian's Interest Group and Webmaster for the Rhode Island Library Association. She is currently on the board of trustees of the South Kingstown, RI Public Library. She has served on the URI Libraries Faculty Development Committee and on the University of Rhode Island Faculty Senate Teaching Effectiveness Committee. She is coauthor of *Teaching Information Literacy: 35 Practical, Standards-based Exercises for College Students* (Chicago: ALA, 2003), andree@uri.edu.

Burkhardt, MacDonald, and Rathemacher were winners of the Outstanding Paper of the Year in *RSR* for the year 2000. Mary C. MacDonald, Andrée J. Rathemacher, and Joanna M. Burkhardt. 2000. "Challenges in Building an Incremental, Multi-year Information Literacy Plan." *RSR: Reference Services Review* 28, no. 3 (August): 240–247.